Karen Leigh Davis

Somali Cats

Everything About Acquisition, Care, Nutrition,
Behavior, Health Care, and Breeding

With 56 Color Photographs

Illustrations by David Wenzel

BARRON'S

All inquiries should be addressed to:
Barron's Educational Series, Inc.
250 Wireless Boulevard
Hauppauge, NY 11788

International Standard Book No. 0-8120-9583-9

Library of Congress Catalog Card No. 95-53672

Library of Congress Cataloging-in-Publication Data
Davis, Karen, 1953–
    Somali Cats : everything about purchase, care, nutrition, breeding, health care, and behavior / Karen Davis : illustrations by David Wenzel.
        p.   cm.—(A complete pet owner's manual)
    Includes bibliographical references and index.
    ISBN 0-8120-9583-9
    1. Somali cat. I. Title. II. Series.
SF449.S65D38   1996
636.8´3—dc20
                                                    95-53672
                                                          CIP
Printed in Hong Kong

987654321

About the Author

Karen Leigh Davis, a professional member of the Cat Writers' Association, has a background in journalism and business writing. She has written a pet care column and numerous feature articles on cats and other companion animals for national and regional magazines and newspapers. As a freelance writer with more than 15 years of experience, she has conducted extensive research on animal-related topics with veterinarians, breeders, and other experts. Davis comes from a cat-loving family and has a lifetime of experience living in the company of cats. She has bred and shown Persians and Himalayans, but she finds all felines, purebred or mixed, domestic or wild, irresistibly charming and beautiful. She lives in Roanoke, Virginia, with four Persian cats.

Front Cover Photo

Grand Champion Regional Winner Tadofa's Mogadishu, a ruddy male Somali owned by Bethany Tod of Cleveland, Ohio, was the national Best-of-Breed winner, CFA's Best Somali, and the Somali Club of America's Cat of the Year for 1993-1994.

Photo Credits

American Greetings Corporation: pages 21, 40, 72, 108 top; Chanan: pages 9 bottom, 13 bottom, 20, 26 top right and bottom, 32, 80 top, 93 top, 100; Donna J. Coss: back cover, inside back cover, pages 28, 29, 37, 44, 52, 53, 61, 76, 77 top and bottom, 80 bottom, 81 top and bottom, 92, 96 top, 109 bottom left and right; Larry Johnson: pages 24, 49, 105; Rob and Jenny Kwolek: front cover; Jane Howard: pages 85, 88, 108 bottom, 112; James E. Mazzone: inside front cover, pages 12 bottom, 96 bottom; Mark McCullough: pages 8 bottom, 9 top; Bob Schwartz: pages 8 top, 13 top, 16, 45, 56, 73, 97 top, 109 top; Gulliver Spring: pages 26 top left, 64, 93 bottom, 97 bottom, 101; Carl Widmer: page 12 top.

Contents

Acknowledgments

I wish to thank my mother, Ruby S. Davis, for her support during the writing of this book; Sally L. Harris for encouraging me to become a writer in the first place; Grace Freedson, Director of Acquisitions, Barron's Educational Series, Inc., for recruiting me; Mary Falcon, Project Editor, for her skillful editing and guidance; James William Poage, D.V.M., and Connie Canode, D.V.M., both of Roanoke, Virginia, for proofreading and correcting selected chapters; Elaine Wexler-Mitchell, D.V.M., of Orange, California, for contributing feline health care information; CFA Somali Breed Council Secretary Karen Talbert (Carquinez Somali Cattery) for furnishing Somali history and breeder information and for submitting photos; Bethany T. Tod (Tadofa Somalis) for providing information and

for introducing me to her charming Somalis; Phillip Sponenberg, D.V.M., Ph.D., of the Virginia-Maryland Regional College of Veterinary Medicine, for simplifying color inheritance for me; Evelyn Mague, International Somali Cat Club, for Somali history and background information; Margot M. Sweet, President, Somali Cat Club of America, for information and photo submissions; CFA Abyssinian Breed Council Secretary Gene Rankin for information regarding the Abyssinian cat; James Richards, D.V.M., of the Cornell Feline Health Center for returning my calls and for answering my endless questions; and author J. Anne Helgren for her helpful suggestions.

Karen Leigh Davis
October, 1995

The most common Somali color is ruddy, burnt-sienna ticked with black.

A History and Description of the Somali Cat

Humble Beginnings

In true Cinderella fashion, the Somali cat rose from humble origins as the unwanted, longhaired stepsister of the Abyssinian cat to a captivating favorite in the show ring hall. The story began in the 1950s, when longhaired kittens started cropping up in North American Abyssinian litters. The Abyssinian cat is a shorthaired breed, and after much hard work to improve its characteristics by selectively mating related cats, most Aby breeders were understandably puzzled by the occasional birth of a fuzzy, longhaired youngster in their purebred litters. To protect their reputations, most kept quiet if one of these unexpected longhairs appeared. They simply gave away the unwanted kitten as a pet without papers and sometimes altered the parents to keep the aberrant gene out of the bloodlines. As a result, no one knows for certain how long the fuzzy anomalies had been showing up in other Aby litters around the world prior to their appearance in North America.

Although interest in breeding the longhaired Abys began at about the same time in the United States, Canada, and Australia, U.S. breeders were the first to push for their acceptance and recognition as a new breed. Now a separate breed in its own right, the Somali cat still is best described as a longhaired Abyssinian, and its history would be remiss without a brief discussion of the Abyssinian's origins.

The Abyssinian Cat

The Abyssinian, a sleek, slender, shorthaired breed, possibly of African origin, is noted for its reddish-brown hair "ticked" with bands of darker color. The ticking, or agouti pattern, results from alternating light- and dark-colored bands on each hair shaft, giving the coat a delicately flecked appearance. The Abyssinian has two or three of these color bands on each hair shaft, whereas a mature Somali's longer hair has an average eight to ten bands. Genetically, Somalis and Abyssinians are a unique form of tabby cat without stripes. Both breeds bear the tabby's characteristic "M" on the forehead, but usually show no visible barring elsewhere on the body. In fact, tabby striping on the body or legs can earn a penalty in the show ring.

One of the oldest known cat breeds, the Abyssinian remarkably resembles the lithe and stately Egyptian cats depicted in ancient paintings and sculptures. With their large, pointed ears and almond-shaped eyes, modern-day Abyssinians, and especially their longhaired Somali sisters with their tufted ears and cheeks, retain the muscular, lynx-like look of the African wildcat, *Felis lybica*. This animal's mummified remains have been found in Egyptian tombs and is believed to be a forerunner of *Felis catus*, today's domestic cat. For these reasons, many people theorize that Abyssinians may be direct descendants of the sacred cats of the Nile.

History credits the ancient Egyptians with being among the first people to domesticate the cat about 3,500 years ago. Because of their immense value in protecting grain stores from rats and mice, cats enjoyed a long period of elevated status in this early civilization. Archaeological discoveries tell us that Egyptians worshipped cats as house-hold gods, mourned their loss when one died, and mummified the remains for entry into the afterlife.

Although recent research suggests that the Abyssinian may have originated along coastal India instead of Egypt, there is no doubt that the breed was refined in England. The breed is named, not for its national origin, but for the first such cat shown in England, a cat named Zula, which was imported from Abyssinia (now Ethiopia) around 1868. American cat fanciers didn't begin actively breeding Abyssinians from imported British stock until the 1930s.

Among the oldest of cat breeds, the Abyssinian closely resembles cats depicted in ancient Egyptian art and sculpture.

The Somali Cat

The Somali possesses the Abyssinian's wild, lithe beauty and agouti coloring with the bonus of a medium-long, silky coat and a foxlike, bushy tail. But how and why the gene that produces a longhaired coat showed up in the shorthaired Abyssinian breed remains a matter of debate. Some argue that the Somali is the result of a spontaneous mutation, in which the shorthair gene simply converted to a longhair gene in a quirk of nature. Others point to the possibility that early Abyssinian outcrosses to other breeds accidentally introduced the longhair gene. Proponents of this theory say that such hybridization most likely occurred some time between the late 1800s and the late

1940s. During this period, the registrations of Abyssinian foundation stock show several cats having at least one parent of unknown origin. In those early days it was accepted practice to use cats of unknown parentage in breeding programs, as long as the cats' appearance met the breed standard. Such a cat could be registered as "foundation" stock only after several cat show judges approved its worthiness as a breed specimen. Later on, the aftermath of World War II in Europe left a critical shortage of pedigreed stock, forcing many breeders to crossbreed their cats to build back their numbers.

Genetics

Regardless of how or when the longhair gene leaked into the bloodlines, once there, producing the Somali cat became simply a matter of

The Somali is basically a longhaired Abyssinian.

genetic roulette. This is because the shorthair gene is dominant, and the longhair gene is recessive. A kitten gets one gene for coat length from each parent. The kitten that inherits a shorthair gene from one parent and a longhair gene from the other will grow up to be a shorthaired cat, even though it carries the hidden longhair gene. This is true in any breed, and because the longhair gene is recessive, it can be handed down unseen through several generations. However, the laws of probability dictate that two shorthaired cats, both carrying the recessive longhair gene, have about a one-in-four chance of eventually producing longhaired offspring. To be born with long hair, a Somali kitten must inherit two of the recessive genes, one from each parent (see Basic Feline Genetics, page 95).

History

Genetics aside, the incomplete ancestry of one foundation-registered female in the Aby bloodlines, named Roverdale Purrkins and born in England during or after World War II, is particularly noteworthy. Because Roverdale Purrkins looked like an Abyssinian in color and coat length, British breeder Janet C. Robertson was able to register her as a foundation Aby and use her to start her Roverdale Cattery. Purrkins possibly could have carried the elusive longhair gene, even though she was a shorthair. Her sire was unknown, and her dam, Mrs. Mews, was an unregistered, agouti-colored feline of unknown ancestry. Moreover, one of Purrkins' descendants, a male Aby named Raby Chuffa, may well have carried the longhair gene to North America in 1952, when he was imported from England by Mrs. Francis Shuler-Taft of the Selene Cattery. This theory seems plausible considering that pedigree studies trace nearly all North American

A ruddy Abyssinian with the characteristic tabby "M" on the forehead.

Somalis back to this single British import.

As Abyssinian popularity grew on both continents, modern selective breeding practices inevitably played a role in creating the Somali. *Linebreeding*, or mating related cats to enhance breed characteristics, increased the opportunities for two longhair-gene-carrying individuals to pair up and produce longhaired offspring.

In those early years, however, the resulting fuzzy-haired kittens no doubt caused quite a stir, partly because they stood out so markedly, being somewhat bigger and darker than their shorthaired siblings. Curiously, they proved to be slower to mature, also, sporting big feet, gangly legs, and no ticking weeks longer, a tendency that still sets Somalis apart from their Abyssinian sisters and brothers. Because of their longer fur, Somali kittens typically do not begin showing their ticking until about four months, and many may not reach their full color for a year or more. Although physically mature by 12 to 18 months, some Somalis still sport an adolescent coat at age two, with their ticking continuing to mature even afterward.

The Somali's late-blooming beauty seemed destined to go unnoticed until about 1968, when a cat named George was surrendered by his owner to a private New Jersey animal shelter. Abyssinian breeder Evelyn Mague, who was the shelter's president at the time, accepted the cat for adoption. As she held George at arm's length and studied his plush coat and rich color, she realized she had a longhaired Aby in her hands. Intrigued, she investigated the cat's background and soon learned that, because he was born the only longhair in a litter of normal shorthaired Abys, he had been given away as a pet. Incredibly, George's sire turned out to be Lynn-Lee's Lord Dublin (nicknamed Dubbies), a stud

This magnificent blue male beautifully displays the Somali's agouti coloring and fox-like, bushy tail.

These fawn (left) and ruddy (right) Somali kittens may not reach their full coat and color for a year or more.

9

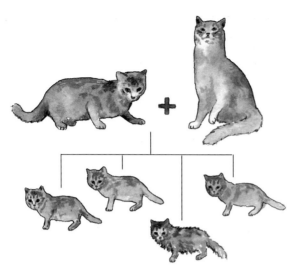

Two shorthaired cats can produce long-haired offspring, if both parents carry the recessive gene for long hair.

from Mague's own breeding program. Even more serendipitous was the discovery that a recent addition to her cattery, Lo-Mi-R's Trill-by (Trilly), was none other than George's dam. Despite his excellent breeding, however, George had fared no better than an ordinary street cat. The poor cat had been through five homes in less than a year without protective shots, so Mague had him vaccinated and neutered and, to give him some value, sold him for $75, the fair market price for a pet-quality Aby in those days.

Realizing now that both of George's parents carried the recessive longhair gene, Mague set out to develop a new breed of longhairs. Because of opposition from other Aby breeders, who wanted to rid their bloodlines of the longhair gene rather than perpetuate it, Mague realized that simply establishing a new, longhaired "variety" of Abyssinians was out of the question at the time. But by developing a new "breed" with a different name, she rea-

soned, other little unwanted longhairs like George could enjoy a better future.

Mague is credited with naming the new breed after modern-day Somalia, which borders the ancient African kingdom of Abyssinia, called Ethiopia today. Eventually, her efforts produced Lynn-Lee's Pollyanna, born January 3, 1972 and generally regarded as the first so-named "Somali" to be shown in the United States, although some other longhairs reportedly were exhibited before, one as early as 1955 as a household pet and one in 1965 as an AOV (Any Other Variety) Abyssinian. In 1972, Mague founded the first Somali Cat Club of America (SCCA). Her diligent work with the longhairs spurred interest among some other U.S. breeders, who also began campaigning for the breed's recognition.

Meanwhile, unknown at first to U.S. breeders, Australian and New Zealand breeders were developing their own breeding programs with Abys imported from England. In Canada, too, the longhaired kittens had not escaped notice. Canadian Cat Association all-breed judge Ken McGill founded the first Somali line in that country after a cat show exhibitor played a good-natured prank on him. For a laugh, Canadian Aby breeder Mary Mailing slipped a longhair into a 1963 Abyssinian class McGill was judging in Calgary. When McGill removed the cat from the judging cage for examination, fellow exhibitors and spectators chuckled at his surprise. But the laugh was on them, because, according to various accounts, McGill was so struck by the cat's beautiful coat and conformation that he asked Mailing for one to breed. He purchased a male kitten named May-Ling Tutseita of Dunedin, whose name now appears on a significant number of Somali pedigrees. McGill quit breeding Somalis after a few years, but Don Richings of the Don-Al Cattery in Canada acquired one of his cats and continued the bloodlines.

Achieving Recognition

For a time, Somali breeding in North America remained concentrated in the eastern United States and Canada while pioneer breeders in both countries collaborated and exchanged information. To promote the breed, they made their Somalis increasingly visible at cat shows, exhibiting them in AOV nonchampionship classes. In these classes, reserved for experimental breeds and AOVS (Any Other Varieties) of existing breeds, judges examine cats that are "discovered" by chance or created through hybridization of existing breeds. The judges award ribbons and talk with breeders about a proposed standard for the new breed or variety. In this way, judges, spectators, and exhibitors see and learn about new feline breeds, colors, or coat types. Practices regarding the acceptance of a new breed vary from one cat-registering association to another, but, in general, a new breed must meet certain criteria before it achieves recognition. Usually, a specified number of the cats have to be registered and shown under provisional status before the breed becomes eligible for championship competition.

Associations

The National Cat Fanciers' Association (NCFA) was the first North American registry to recognize the Somali around 1974–75, the first season the SCCA presented awards. The Cat Fanciers' Federation (CFF) soon followed with recognition in 1975. By 1977, the breed held championship status in the Canadian Cat Association (CCA) and the American Cat Fanciers' Association (ACFA). The world's largest registry, the Cat Fanciers' Association (CFA), granted provisional status in 1977, then advanced the breed to championship competition in May, 1979. Also in 1979, The International Cat Association (TICA) was incorporated and recognized the Somali from the outset. By 1980, when the American Cat Association (ACA) finally admitted the Somali to its championship ranks, all North American cat registries had officially recognized the breed. In addition, two new U.S. registries, the American Association of Cat Enthusiasts (AACE) and the United Feline Organization (UFO), have recognized Somalis since their charters began in 1993 and 1995, respectively.

These associations not only register cats, they also verify the pedigrees and set rules for breeding and showing. The pedigree of a purebred cat lists several generations of its recorded ancestors. In addition to maintaining stud books, the associations sanction shows, present awards, charter clubs, train judges and approve breed standards (see the chapter, Showing Your Somali, beginning on page 83).

The Somali Today

In a short time, the Somali progressed from its humble origins as an unwanted recessive gene product to its cherished status among the "cat fancy" (the term describing those involved in breeding or showing cats). In 1976, the first Somali won the highly coveted award of Best Cat at a championship show. Fittingly, the cat was Lynn-Lee's Christopher, bred by Evelyn Mague, and a brother (same parents, different litter) to George, the shelter cat that launched Mague's pioneer interest in the breed. As a testament to the breed's popularity, Somali breeders now reside across the entire United States, as well as in Europe, Japan, and, as mentioned, Canada, Australia, and New Zealand. Because Somali litters are small, breeders

Ear tufts and a full neck ruff add to the lush appearance of the Somali's coat.

The Somali color red is called "sorrel" by some cat associations.

typically maintain waiting lists of potential buyers wanting kittens.

Despite its small numbers, however, the Somali today holds a firm middle ground among all pedigreed cats and is the sixth most popular longhaired breed in terms of annual new registrations. In 1994, 20 years after its initial acceptance, the Somali ranked sixteenth in popularity out of 37 breeds, according to CFA registration totals. That year, 523 Somali cats were registered with CFA, down from 591 registered in 1993. The decline, experts say, reflects an overall downward trend in new registrations for all breeds noted since 1990.

The Somali Breed Standard

A breed standard is a written blueprint describing the ideal conformation and coloring of animals representing that breed. Every cat competing in a show is judged according to how well it meets the written standard for its breed. For use in their breeding programs, conscientious breeders try to select cats that most closely fit the standard or that possess enough of the desired qualities to promise outstanding offspring. Ideally, their aim is to breed the best to the best, whenever possible.

Colors

Selective breeding sometimes results in new colors that may be added to the standard after meeting certain criteria for acceptance. At first, the Somali standard accepted only two colors: ruddy, the most common color, and red, sometimes called sorrel or cinnamon. Today, all North American registries recognize Somalis in two other colors: blue and fawn. In 1986, CFA accepted blue Somalis for championship status. By 1990, the rare fawn-colored Somalis achieved recognition. ACA, the oldest cat association, also accepts lilac and cream Somalis.

Although silver and its variations—cinnamon silver, blue silver, chocolate silver, etc.—are accepted colors in some European countries, the only U.S. registries currently recognizing silver Somalis are NCFA, AACE, and UFO. Recently, TICA accepted silver Abyssinians, but not yet silver Somalis, in its New Breed and Color (NBC) category. However, the largest registry, CFA, disqualifies any Abyssinian or Somali color other than the accepted four: ruddy, red, blue, and fawn.

Size

As noted, policies and standards within the United States vary from one cat-registering association to the other, and committees convene periodically to amend and update them. Just as breed standards in foreign countries may accept many colors not recognized in the U.S., they may vary in other ways as well. For example, U.S. standards call for a medium to large Somali, whereas, in Denmark, judges reportedly prefer slightly smaller cats. In most instances, however, breed standards for Somali build and body "type" retain significant similarities from country to country. If you're interested in showing, write to the appropriate association(s) and request their most current information (see Useful Addresses and Literature in the back of this book).

CFA Somali Show Standard (1995–96)

In the show ring, a Somali is judged on how closely it fits the ideal standard adopted by the association governing the show. Points are assigned for various features, with a total score of 100 possible, but rare. The following table compares the CFA point scores allowed for Somalis and Abyssinians.

According to the table, coat is worth more in the Somali standard (20 points versus 10), while in the Abyssinian standard, color is weighted more heavily.

Black silver kitten. Silver Somalis are accepted in only a few cat associations.

Blue Somalis like this one sport an ivory-oatmeal ground color ticked with slate blue.

13

CFA Point Scores

Feature	Points	
	Somali	*Abyssinian*
Head:	(25)	(25)
Skull	6	6
Muzzle	6	6
Ears	7	7
Eye Shape	6	6
Body:	(25)	(30)
Torso	10	15
Legs and feet	10	10
Tail	5	5
Coat:	(20)	(10)
Texture	10	10
Length	10	—
Color:	(30)	(35)
Color	10	15
Markings	5	—
Ticking	10	15
Eye color	5	5

CFA's standard for Somalis is included here because it is the world's largest registry of pedigreed cats.

General: The overall impression of the Somali is that of a well-proportioned, medium-to-large cat, firm muscular development, lithe, showing an alert, lively interest in all surroundings, with an even disposition and easy to handle. The cat is to give the appearance of activity, sound health, and general vigor.

Head: A modified, slightly rounded wedge without flat planes, the brow, cheek, and profile lines all showing a gentle contour. A slight rise from the bridge of the nose to the forehead, which should be of good size with width between the ears flowing into the arched neck without a break.

Muzzle: Shall follow gentle contours in conformity with the skull, as viewed from the front profile. Chin shall be full, neither undershot nor overshot, having a rounded appearance. The muzzle shall not be sharply pointed and there shall be no evidence of snippiness (too narrow), foxiness (too long), or whisker pinch (pushed up at the nose, causing a snarling expression). Allowance to be made for jowls in adult males.

Ears: Large, alert, moderately pointed, broad and cupped at the base. Ear set on a line toward the rear of the skull. The inner ear shall have horizontal tufts that reach nearly to the other side of the ear; tufts desirable.

Eyes: Almond-shaped, large, brilliant, and expressive. Skull aperture neither round nor oriental. Eyes accented by dark lidskin encircled by light-colored area. Above each a short dark vertical pencil stroke with a dark pencil line continuing from the upper lid toward the ear.

Body: Torso medium long, lithe, and graceful, showing well-developed muscular strength. Rib cage is rounded; back is slightly arched giving the appearance of a cat about to spring; flank level with no tuck up. Conformation strikes a medium between the extremes of cobby and svelte lengthy types.

Legs and Feet: Legs in proportion to torso; feet oval and compact. When standing, the Somali gives the impression of being nimble and quick. Toes: five in front and four in back.

Tail: Having a full brush, thick at the base and slightly tapering. Length in balance with torso.

Coat: Texture very soft to the touch, extremely fine and double-coated. The more dense the coat, the better. Length: a medium-length coat, except over shoulders, where a slightly shorter length is permitted. Preference is to be given to a cat with ruff and breeches, giving a full-coated appearance to the cat. (Such preference applies when all other points between competing cats are equal.)

Penalize: Color faults—cold gray or sandy tone to coat color; mottling or speckling on unticked areas. Pattern faults—necklaces, leg bars, tabby stripes or bars on body; lack of desired markings on head and tail. Black roots on body.

Disqualify: White locket or groin spot or white anywhere on body other than on the upper throat, chin, or nostrils. Any skeletal abnormality. Wrong color paw pads or nose leather. Any other colors than the four accepted colors. Unbroken necklace. Incorrect number of toes. Kinks in tail.

Somali Colors

Coat Color: Warm and glowing. *Ticking:* distinct and even, with dark-colored bands contrasting with light-colored bands on the hair shafts. Undercoat color clear and bright to the skin. Deeper color shades desired; however, intensity of ticking not to be sacrificed for depth of color. Darker shading along spine continuing

The agouti pattern. Alternating bands of light and dark colors on the hair shafts give the Somali coat its characteristic ticking.

through tip of tail. Darker shading up the hocks, also shading allowed at the point of the elbow. Preference given to cats UNMARKED on the undersides, chest, and legs; tail without rings. *Facial markings:* dark lines extending from eyes and brows, cheekbone shading, dots and shading on whisker pads are all desirable enhancements. Eyes accentuated by fine dark line, encircled by light-colored area. *Eye color:* gold or green, the more richness and depth of color the better.

Ruddy: Ground color burnt-sienna, ticked with various shades of darker brown or black, the extreme outer tip to be the darkest. Tail tipped with black. The underside and inside of legs to be a tint to harmonize with the ground color. *Nose leather:* tile red. *Paw pads:* black or dark brown, with black between toes, extending slightly beyond the paws.

Red: Ground color rich, warm, glowing red, ticked with chocolate-brown, the extreme outer tip to be

darkest. Tail tipped with chocolate-brown. The underside and inside of legs to be a tint to harmonize with the ground color. *Nose leather:* rosy pink. *Paw pads:* pink, with chocolate-brown between toes, extending slightly beyond the paws.

Blue: Ground color ivory-oatmeal, ticked with various shades of slate blue, the extreme outer tip to be the darkest. Tail tipped with slate blue. The underside and inside of legs to be a warm blush-beige/apricot to harmonize with the ground color. *Nose leather:* old rose. *Paw pads:* mauve, with slate blue between toes, extending slightly beyond the paws.

Fawn: Ground color warm rose-beige, ticked with light cocoa-brown, the extreme outer tip to be the darkest. Tail tipped with light cocoa-brown. The underside and inside of legs to be a tint to harmonize with the ground color. *Nose leather:* salmon. *Paw pads:* pink with light cocoa-brown between the toes, extending slightly beyond the paws.

The rare but lovely fawn Somali is a paler version of red.

Somali Temperament

Often described as natural show-offs and born clowns, Somali cats are extroverted, athletic, active, and alert. Their remarkable intelligence, playful curiosity, and happy disposition make them particularly alluring and captivating as companions. They thrive on lots of attention, readily seek human company, and demand to be treated as one of the family.

Acquiring Your Somali

Before You Buy

Although unpedigreed "alley" cats make just as good companions as purebred felines, acquiring a Somali has some special advantages. Because a purebred has a recorded ancestry, certain qualities, such as temperament and appearance, are more predictable. But as you consider getting a Somali—or any cat—remember that your new relationship could last as long as a decade or two. For greatest compatibility, the cat you select as your long-term friend must suit your personality and lifestyle.

Noted for their high energy levels, Somalis retain their playfulness long past kittenhood. Active, intelligent, and curious, their amusing antics may occasionally exasperate you. They can learn to pry open doors, get into cabinets and drawers, and even turn on water faucets! Some owners report that their Somalis have a particular fascination with water and love to play under dripping spouts. With paws as busy and agile as a monkey's, they may take great delight in unrolling toilet paper and paper towels. If such occasional mischief makes you cringe instead of chuckle, perhaps one of the more sedate cat breeds would be a better choice. Before you commit, know what you want in a cat companion. To help you decide, consider the following:

Show Cat or Pet?

Breeders price and sell Somalis according to whether they are show-quality, breeder-quality, or pet-quality. Cats in all three categories are purebred and fully registrable in the cat associations.

Show-quality Somalis are the most expensive to buy because their breeders think they are outstanding examples of the breed, based on the standard, and will perform well in the show ring. Few breeders will sell a "top-show" cat to a novice. But many will part with proven winners retired from breeding if the buyer agrees to spay or neuter and show the cat in alter classes. This way, the buyer gets a high-quality show cat without the hassle of owning an intact animal. Buy only from breeders with a proven track record in the show ring. Study pedigrees carefully. The more grand champion titles that appear in the first two or three generations of a kitten's ancestry, the better the chances that it, too, may become a winner. It's important to note, however, that Somali kittens develop slowly in coat and color, and picking a winner early is not a sure science. Born with dark, nearly black shading, Somali kittens lighten to their ticked color after about 15 weeks. Some may take a year or two to sport their full color and coat. Others pleasantly surprise even their breeders when undesirable white markings fade completely with maturity. Because Somalis change so much as they grow, it is wise to purchase a show-quality kitten when it's a little older—at five or six months. Although price varies greatly, depending on availability and geographical location, expect to pay from $800 to $2,000 for a show-quality red or ruddy Somali kitten. The rarer blues and fawns may cost from $1,500 to $6,000.

Breeder-quality Somalis are classified accordingly because they fail to

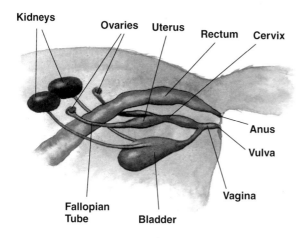

Kidneys

Ovaries Uterus

Rectum Cervix

Anus

Vulva

Vagina

Fallopian
Tube

Bladder

Spaying safely removes a female cat's ovaries, tubes, and uterus so that she cannot have kittens.

meet the show standard in some small way, yet they possess enough good qualities—one of which is usually an excellent pedigree—to potentially produce outstanding offspring. Breeder-quality kittens typically sell for slightly less than their show-quality littermates. Expect to pay between $650 and $800 for a breeder-quality red or ruddy kitten, and more for blues or fawns.

Pet-quality Somalis are the most affordable, because some minor cosmetic flaw, such as a white groin spot, makes them unsuitable for show ring competition but ideal for household companions. The pet-quality designation in no way means that a Somali in this category is less healthy or less desirable to own. In fact, most people, except for judges and breeders, cannot distinguish a pet-quality Somali from a grand champion. So, unless you intend to show or breed Somalis, a pet-quality Somali is your smartest buy. Expect to pay from $400 for a pet-quality Somali, depending on availability and geographical location.

Responsible breeders sell their pet-quality kittens with a signed agreement that the new owner will spay or neuter. To ensure that the agreement is honored, the seller usually elects to withhold the kitten's "papers," or registration slip, until the buyer furnishes a veterinary statement proving that the required operation has been performed. The purpose of such an agreement is to discourage unethical people from buying purebred cats at pet prices, then breeding them for profit and adding to an already overcrowded pet population.

One Cat or Two?

If you work away from home all day and must leave your Somali alone for long periods, consider getting two kittens so they can keep each other company. If you cannot afford to buy two purebreds, consider adopting a kitten from your local animal shelter. Mixed-breed cats make excellent pets as well as suitable companions for Somalis. If you intend to show, remember, too, that mixed-breeds and part-Somalis can be exhibited at cat shows in the household pet category, where cats are judged according to their beauty, condition, and personality, rather than the breed standard. If your budget and living accommodations allow it, acquiring two kittens will double your pleasure and may even prevent destructive feline behaviors that develop out of boredom and loneliness.

Kitten Versus Adult Cat?

Most people understandably do not want to miss the cute kitten stage. However, acquiring a grown cat has some cost-effective benefits if it already has been altered and is up-to-date on its vaccinations. Adult cats often cost less than kittens, too, particularly if they are being retired early from a breeding program or from the show ring and simply need a good home. Although kittenhood holds special joys for cat lovers, it can be the most destructive stage. Kittens aren't born knowing how you expect them to behave in your home. They have to be properly socialized and taught what adult cats may already know: that they cannot claw your clothing, climb up your pants leg, swing on your draperies, or sharpen claws on the couch. On the other hand, you won't know whether an adult cat has behavior problems related to its past care and training, unless you trust the seller's word and reputation.

Male Versus Female

If you intend to breed Somalis, start with the best quality female you can find. Otherwise, both sexes make equally fine companions. If you are not going to breed, then you definitely will want to alter your Somali when it reaches an appropriate age. Many veterinarians recommend that males be neutered between eight and ten months of age and that females be spayed at six months. However, to discourage indiscriminate breeding, some Somali breeders elect to spay between 12 and 14 weeks and neuter between 10 and 12 weeks before selling their pet-quality kittens. Studies indicate that early spaying and neutering is safe and does not adversely affect feline maturity, as once thought.

Because spaying involves opening the abdomen to remove the female's ovaries, tubes, and uterus, this operation costs more than neutering, a simpler procedure that removes the male's testicles. Remember, however, that the one-time cost of spaying a female is still considerably less than the cumulative cost of raising and finding homes for litter after litter of kittens. If cost concerns you, ask your breeder, veterinarian, or local animal shelter about low-cost spay and neuter programs available in your area.

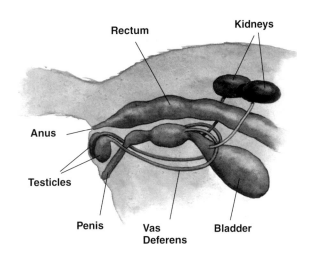

Neutering a male cat reduces or eliminates undesirable spraying behaviors.

Both operations reduce an animal's natural desire to roam in search of mates, making it a nicer pet and improving its chances of living a longer, healthier life. Roaming animals are more likely to be killed by cars, injured in fights, or exposed to diseases. Repeated veterinary bills for pets injured while roaming and fighting can quickly exceed the one-time cost of spaying or neutering. Spaying eliminates the female's bothersome heat periods along with her ability to become pregnant. The operation also eliminates the possibility of any disease or infections in the organs removed and decreases the chance of breast cancer occurring later in life. Neutering the male reduces aggressive behaviors, eliminates testicular diseases, and decreases the chance of prostate cancer later in life, as well as diseases in other glands affected by male hormones. Neutering also curbs a male's undesirable tendency to spray urine in the house to mark his territory. Contrary to popular myth, your Somali will not grow fat and lazy

Somalis share a fascination with water and love to play with dripping faucets.

not allowing intact cats to roam freely and breed indiscriminately.

To determine whether a kitten is a male or a female, raise the tail and look at the rear end. In the female, the genital opening looks like a small slit and appears directly below the anus. In the male, the anus and penis are spaced farther apart, and both openings are round.

Friends' and/or Family Allergies

Consider the people who no longer may be able to visit your home because their asthma or allergies become aggravated when in the presence of a cat. You don't want to acquire a cat, only to give it up later because your social life suffers. Proteins produced by the cat's salivary and sebaceous glands trigger the allergic response when they are deposited on the cat's fur during grooming, then dry and flake into tiny particles that can be easily inhaled. The particles settle primarily in carpets, draperies, upholstered furniture, mattresses, walls, and ceilings.

For the person who experiences only mild or intermittent allergy symptoms, certain compromises may allow a comfortable coexistence with cats. Suggested coping strategies include vacuuming frequently, replacing carpets with hard floors, replacing upholstered furniture with vinyl or leather, washing the cat in distilled water once a month, applying anti-allergy wipes or sprays to the cat's fur, using an air purifier in the home, and keeping ductwork, furnace, and air-conditioning filters clean. Allergy medications and desensitizing allergy shots help in many cases. And soon, a new vaccine, currently undergoing clinical trials, may provide relief for people allergic to cats.

After you've decided whether you want a male or female Somali, show cat or pet, one cat or two, kitten or

after being spayed or neutered. Only too much food and too little exercise will cause that.

Aside from the health and behavior benefits, spaying or neutering your pet Somali is simply the right thing to do. Why? Because an average size litter of five kittens will mature within a year to reproduce about five more kittens apiece. In simple arithmetic, that's 25 kittens in one year, originating from a single litter. Those 25 cats, if left unaltered, can reproduce five more apiece, adding up to 125, and so on. Of those 125, only a few will be lucky enough to find loving homes. The rest will be surplus, unwanted animals. What happens to them? About 75 percent of cats taken into U.S. shelters are euthanatized each year, with annual figures fluctuating from a staggering 4.3 million to nearly 9.5 million since 1985. Countless others fall victim to the hazards of life in the wild. Because there simply aren't enough homes to go around for so many cats, responsible cat owners and breeders realize it is their moral duty to control this tragic surplus by having pets altered and by adult, consider one final, important point: Are you prepared to take care of your Somali for the rest of its life?

Your Lifestyle

Acquiring a Somali, or any cat, demands a commitment that lasts long after the adorable kitten grows up. And like people, adult cats eventually grow old and may develop special needs. Because cats can live an average 10 to 15 years or more, it is important to look ahead into your own future and ask yourself whether you'll be willing and able to provide your Somali with shelter, food, and regular veterinary care for a decade or two. Of course, it's impossible to predict and plan for every contingency. But if you antici-pate, for example, that you might have to move a long distance within the next few years because of your job, per-haps you'd better postpone getting a Somali, unless you intend to take it with you.

Housing situation: Be certain, too, that your housing situation is suitable for owning a pet. Whether you rent or own your home, certain restrictions may prohibit or limit the kind and num-ber of animals you can keep. Landlords usually require a pet dam-age deposit, in case your cat claws the draperies or carpets. This is not unreasonable, because, as a cat owner, you are liable and responsible for any property damages, as well as any personal injuries your cat may cause. To avoid possible difficulties, find out what rules and regulations, if any, apply in your area, and assess your ability to fully comply, before you acquire a Somali.

Travel: Consider your lifestyle before deciding to get a Somali. For example, if you travel often, do you have a trusted friend or relative who is willing to care for your Somali while you're away? If not, can you afford the frequent expense of boarding facilities

If you can afford it, acquiring two kittens doubles your pleasure. They also provide each other with companionship while you're away at work. (Photo courtesy of American Greetings Corporation, © AGC, Inc.)

and pet-sitting services in your area? Can you afford veterinary care, and do you have time to give your cat the love and attention it needs and deserves?

Your age and health: While most people expect to outlive their pets, this is never a certainty. What would hap-pen to your Somali if you died first? Or who would take care of your Somali if you suddenly became inca-pacitated by an injury or illness? Too often, an animal faces neglect, abuse, or abandonment if the owner hasn't planned ahead for its care in case of such emergencies. If you live alone, someone needs to have advance instructions—and keys—to enter your property immediately and assume care of your Somali if you die or become disabled. Providing for your cat in your will isn't as unusual or as difficult as it may sound. Yet, many owners never think of it. In 1994, the Association of the Bar of the City of New York published an informative

Sexing kittens: In females (right), the genital opening looks like a small slit. In males, the genital opening is round and is located farther below the anus than in the female.

brochure titled "Providing for Your Pets in the Event of Your Death or Hospitalization" (see Useful Addresses and Literature in the back of this book). The pamphlet, among the first of its kind, simplifies some of the legalities involved and recommends leaving your cat outright to a friend or relative who agrees to comply with your wishes. You then name that person as your cat's guardian in your will. You also may wish to bequeath a modest sum of money to that person to cover the cost of cat care. Consult a lawyer for advice.

Acquiring a cat, like having children, will change your life and should never be undertaken without some forethought, planning, and preparation. Lots of people dash out and buy baby books as soon as they learn they're expecting a child. Reading about the selection, care, and training of the new feline companion who will share the next 15 years or so of your life should be no less important.

Finding a Breeder

Once you've decided to buy a Somali, you need to know where to look to find a reputable breeder. If you live in or near a large city, chances are good that you will find a small-volume breeder within driving distance of your home. Otherwise, you may have to search out-of-state and consider having a kitten shipped to you. Attending cat shows is the best way to meet breeders and see the quality of their cats. You also can learn a great deal about cat care and grooming by visiting shows and talking with the exhibitors. Cat fanciers' magazines list upcoming cat shows and publish breeder directories. The cat-registering associations also can refer you to breeders in or near your area (see Useful Addresses and Literature in the back of this book). Some breeders advertise in the classified sections of newspapers and trade magazines or pin their business cards on bulletin boards at veterinarians' offices.

Because Somalis are a relatively rare breed, you may have to put your name on a waiting list for a kitten, once you've located a breeder. Most people who raise them have only a few litters of kittens each year. But even if you have to wait, small-volume breeders are still a better source than pet shops. For one reason, you're unlikely to find Somalis in pet stores, because of their rarity. In addition, pet shops, particularly those in large malls, typically charge more than independent breeders because they have high rent and overhead. You also cannot see the kitten's parents or examine the environment in which it was reared. However, if, by chance, you do find a Somali in a pet shop, ask the store owner or manager for the breeder's name and telephone number so you can investigate the kitten's background more thoroughly before you consider buying it. If the proprietor seems reluctant to share this information, look elsewhere.

Avoid pet shop stock that comes from kitten mills and "backyard" breeders. Both producers are interested in raising animals only for profit, and their kittens may not be healthy or free of genetic defects. You want to find a conscientious breeder who is committed to improving the Somali breed's aesthetic qualities in terms of genetics, temperament, and appearance. This kind of breeder is usually involved in showing Somalis in addition to breeding them.

Breeders' Questions to You

When you first talk to any breeder, you can gauge how much he cares about his Somalis by the kind of questions he asks you. For example, you've found a responsible breeder if he asks you about other cats you've owned, what you fed them, how often you took them to the veterinarian, and what ultimately happened to them. A conscientious breeder will ask what you're looking for in a new cat, if you want an indoor or outdoor cat, and if you intend to spay or neuter it. Any breeder who questions prospective buyers this closely clearly cares more about what kind of home his or her kittens will go to than about how much money will be made on the sale. The breeder is likely to be equally conscientious about the kittens' health care and proper socialization.

Your Questions to the Breeder

Likewise, you should ask the breeder what vaccinations the kitten has received, what cat association(s) the breeder registers with, and whether his or her cats are free from feline leukemia virus (FeLV) and feline immunodeficiency virus (FIV). Find out how much human handling the kitten has been accustomed to. Experts believe that kittens gently handled a lit-

Attending cat shows is a fun and easy way to meet reputable breeders, see their Somalis, and learn about cat care in general.

tle each day from about age three weeks on grow up to be more people-oriented and better socialized than those that have no human contact at all. If possible, visit the cattery and note its overall cleanliness. If the cattery is too far away, ask to see pictures of the kitten and both parents.

Taking Home the Kitten

A responsible breeder will not let you take home a Somali kitten until it is at least 12 to 16 weeks old. By this time, a kitten has been weaned and litter trained, is eating solid food and has had most or all of its vaccinations. Kittens taken away too young from their original surroundings sometimes suffer from stress and have trouble adjusting to a new environment.

In addition, if your kitten has to be shipped to you, three to four months conforms with most airline age requirements. The breeder usually helps with shipping arrangements, but you can expect to pay all costs, including the airline-approved carrier the kitten will be shipped in. Costs vary, of course, depending on the airline and on the flight distance.

Healthy Somali kittens like these have bright-eyed, alert expressions, clean, shiny coats, and curious, playful dispositions.

Choosing a Healthy Somali

Once you've found a breeder, check the following:

• The kitten you select should have good muscle tone, bright, clear eyes, and an alert, playful personality.

• A healthy kitten should not sneeze or show mucus discharge around the eyes or nose.

• The ears should be clean and free of dark, crusty wax. Head-shaking or ear-scratching may indicate ear mites or other infections.

• The anus should be clean and free of any signs of diarrhea.

• The kitten's coat and environment should be clean and free of fleas. To inspect the coat for fleas, rub your hand against the fur and look for fine grains of black dirt, which is really flea excrement. Flea signs are more prevalent behind the ears, on the back, and at the tail base, where the kitten cannot easily reach to lick clean (see page 57 for a discussion on fleas).

• Tempt the kitten with a feather or ribbon and see how playful and relaxed it is around strangers. If it appears fearful, hisses at you, cringes from your hand or, in general, seems unused to being handled, look elsewhere for a better socialized kitten.

The Somali standard calls for large, alert, moderately pointed ears. Ears focused forward and eyes opened wide indicate that these cats feel a friendly interest in their surroundings.

The overall appearance of the Somali is that of a well-proportioned, medium-to-large cat, lithe and graceful, with a lively expression.

A breeder may rightfully withhold the registration form until you furnish proof that your kitten has been spayed or neutered.

The Sales Agreement

A written sales contract describes all terms of the sale, including the purchase price and payment schedule, the breeder's health guarantee, and any neuter/spay agreement. Contracts vary from breeder to breeder, of course, but all agreements should spell out the buyer's option to return the kitten and get his or her money back if the kitten is found to be unhealthy or unsuitable within a specified period after purchase.

The breeder's contract also may require the kitten's new owner to give the breeder the first option to buy back the kitten, if the new owner can no longer keep it. Some may even include provisions against declawing the cat or selling it to a pet shop. Monetary damages may be awarded if the breeder later learns that the buyer has violated any part of the agreement. Make sure you read and fully understand all terms of the contract before you sign.

Health records and vaccination certificates should accompany the sales agreement. To save money, some breeders vaccinate their own kittens, which is a legal practice.

However, in areas where rabies shots are required for cats, the vaccine usually must be administered in the presence of a state authority, such as a veterinarian or an animal control officer, before a legal certificate can be issued. When shipping kittens by air, health and rabies certificates often are required, depending on the destination and on the airline's regulations.

In addition to health certificates, the purchase price includes the kitten's papers and pedigree. However, if the cat is pet-quality, the sales agreement may stipulate that the animal not be used for breeding. Under such terms, the breeder may rightfully withhold the registration papers until the buyer furnishes proof that the cat has been spayed or neutered.

The Registration Form

After the breeder sends you the kitten's registration slip (see Registering the Litter, page 104), simply fill it out with the name you have chosen for your Somali. Complete the owner information section and mail the form with the proper fee to the association(s) where the breeder registered your kitten's litter. The breeder will have completed the sections on your kitten's breed, sex, hair length, eye color, coat color, etc. Also, if the breeder has a cattery name, it will be printed on the line where you write in your kitten's new name. This cattery name will be part of your kitten's official, registered name. Most forms direct you to select two or three names, in case your first-choice name already has been used by someone else. When the association receives the form, it will verify the pedigree information, approve your name selection, then send you back an owner's certificate.

Bringing Your Somali Home

Preparing for the New Arrival

Resilient by nature, Somalis adapt easily to new people and surroundings. They generally get along well with other cats and even dogs. Still, a little planning and preparation will make your Somali's transition to its new home much easier for all involved, particularly if you have children and other pets. First, pick up some cat food and basic pet supplies to make the kitten's arrival as comfortable as possible. Following are some items you'll need:

Cat carrier: Purchase a suitable cat carrier to bring your kitten home in. Most veterinarians' offices sell inexpensive cardboard carriers, while pet stores carry the sturdier plastic ones, the wicker baskets, and the canvas totebag varieties. If shipping your Somali by air, you will need an airline-approved pet carrier. Regardless of the carrier type you select, it should close securely, be well-ventilated, and roomy enough for a cat to stand and turn around.

Furthermore, each cat in the household needs its own carrier for safe transport to the veterinary clinic or boarding facility. Never put two cats together in a single carrier, even if they are best friends. The tight, unfamiliar quarters might stress them and spur a fight.

Food and water bowls: Every pet in the household needs its own, separate feeding dish. Show the new arrival to its dish, and establish a feeding routine the first day. If other pets try to eat the newcomer's food, feed the kitten in a separate area.

Although more expensive, stainless steel or glass pet bowls have some definite advantages over plastic dishes. They can be sterilized in a dishwasher, whereas plastic dishes may melt. Some cats are sensitive to chemicals in plastic dishes and, with prolonged exposure, may develop feline acne and allergies, conditions evidenced by itchy bald spots and crusty sores around the mouth and nose. Ceramic dishes come in decorative varieties, but select only those sold for human use or labeled lead-free. Otherwise, you have no way of knowing whether the paint and glaze used on the dish contains harmful lead that may leach into the food or water.

Many cats seem to prefer flat, shallow saucers to deep bowls, perhaps

Self-feeders and self-watering containers handily dispense food and water for your Somali while you're away.

Your Somali needs a well-ventilated carrier for trips to the veterinarian.

water or kibble with its paws simply to watch the liquid bubble or the food fall, you'll have to resort to the single-meal dishes, unless, of course, you don't mind the mess.

Litter boxes: Provide one litter box per cat in your household, even if your cats go outdoors. For a kitten's shorter legs, start with a shallow litter pan, then switch to a larger size as the cat grows. By the time your Somali is old enough to go to its new home, it already should know how to use a litter box. After the first few meals in its new home, simply show the kitten to its new litter box, and the instinctive digging and covering behaviors should come naturally.

Pet stores and mail-order catalogs carry a wide variety of litter pans, from the basic open plastic models to the fancy ones with ventilated bottoms and pull-out trays. The more expensive ventilated designs allow air to circulate beneath a litter tray to help dry the urine. Covered litter pans help contain odors and give shy cats privacy, but some cats seem to dislike the confinement. Whatever kind you select, it's important to keep the box clean, or the cat may stop using it if it becomes too soiled (see pages 70–71 for a discussion of litter box problems).

Use a sturdy litter scoop to shovel out the solid wastes each day. Once a week, dump the soiled litter, wash the pan with hot water, and refill with fresh litter. To control odor, stir in a box of baking soda, or try one of many cat box odor control products on the market.

For privacy, place the litter box in a quiet area that has limited noise and foot traffic; however, do not place it too near the cat's food dishes or sleeping quarters. Would you want to eat or sleep next to a toilet?

Kitty litter: The type of litter you select is important, because if your cat doesn't like it, it may refuse to use the

because they don't like their sensitive whiskers to rub the sides of the dish as they eat. Some cats dislike this unpleasant sensation so much that they will resort to scooping the food morsels out with their paws and eating off the floor. Also, select dishes that are heavy enough not to slide across the floor as the cat eats. Wash feeding bowls after meals, and replenish water daily. In hot weather, add a few ice cubes to the water as a cool treat.

Self-feeders: Many owners prefer to offer dry food free-choice for their cats to nibble on throughout the day. Self-feeders handily dispense food from a bulk hopper as the cat eats. The hopper contents usually last a couple of days, making the feeders convenient for leaving out enough food when you are away overnight. Similarly, self-waterers dispense water from an inverted bottle into a dish as the cat drinks. Be warned, however, that some Somalis may view these containers as irresistible playthings. Once your cat discovers the joys of shoveling out box. Some cats don't like the perfumed or chemically treated pellets added to commercial litters to please the nose of human consumers. The cat that stands on the sides of the box, steps gingerly in and out, or rarely digs in the litter, may be telling you that it dislikes the cat box filler. For these finicky types, plain, untreated clay litter, sand, or even dirt may be better choices. You may need to test several fillers to find one that seems to suit the cat.

To aid in sanitation and odor control, some filler brands form solid clumps when moistened with urine so that wet spots scoop out easily with the feces, leaving behind only clean, fresh litter. On the downside, some clumping varieties tend to stick to the fur of long-haired cats; however, many manufacturers have attempted to resolve this consumer complaint. For greater economy, certain litter brands can be rinsed and reused. "Trackless" litter varieties tend to stick less to the paws, reducing the number of granules tracked outside the box onto carpets and floors. Unless labeled as such, most litters are not flushable in modern toilets and septic systems.

Grooming supplies: Buy nail clippers, a wide-toothed, steel comb and the best quality soft, natural bristle brush you can afford. For kittens, start with small and medium-size steel combs, and save the wide-toothed one for use on full, adult coats. For flea control, purchase a fine-toothed comb. Once caught in the comb's closely-spaced teeth, fleas drown easily when dipped in a pan of water. A fine comb also readily removes flea dirt deep in the fur. Talcum or baby powder helps remove oil and dirt from a cat's coat when sprinkled in and brushed out completely. For bathing your Somali, select a pet shampoo labeled as safe for use on cats. Avoid dishwashing detergents, laundry soaps, or human shampoos. Don't use dog shampoos,

Some Somalis enjoy a round, cozy "snuggle" bed of their own, while others prefer sleeping on the owner's bed.

because the ingredients may be too harsh and concentrated for cats. For tips on grooming your Somali, refer to the chapter on Grooming, beginning on page 76.

Cat beds: Many owners spend lots of money on fancy pet beds only to have their cats refuse to use them. More than likely your Somali will prefer to sleep on your bed or in your favorite chair. Some cats like to sleep in high places; others like deep baskets or dark hideaways. Some like to sprawl on their backs in a ray of sunshine spilling through a window or glass door. Most like to snuggle in soft, plush fabrics. Whether you provide a blanket or buy a cat bed, select a material that can be laundered frequently, yet still retain its softness.

Scratching posts: Cats have an innate need to scratch and sharpen their claws. Even declawed cats exhibit this instinctive behavior, which not only removes dead nail and reconditions the claws but also marks territory with scent from glands in the paw pads.

Before bringing your Somali home, you may want to purchase a cat tree or scratching post, a cat carrier, cat food, food and water bowls, a few cat toys, . . .

. . . a litter box, a bag of kitty litter, a litter scoop, . . .

. . . and grooming supplies.

The scent draws the cat back to the same scratching spot time after time. To prevent your Somali from clawing your furniture, provide it with an alternative scratching post. Select a carpet-covered post available at pet shops, or build your own. Make sure the base is wide enough and the post stable enough not to rock back and forth or tip over as the cat claws it. If the post falls over and frightens the cat, it may refuse to use it again. The post also needs to be tall enough to allow a full-grown cat standing on its hind legs to stretch upward to its full length.

Carpeted cat trees that extend from floor to ceiling make attractive scratching posts and come in all colors to match any room's decor. Because Somalis like high places, they especially enjoy the exercise and climbing opportunities these trees offer. Creative designs incorporate built-in perches and peekaboo condos for cat-napping. Pet stores can order cat trees for you through catalogs, if they don't keep them in stock. Because Somalis like to be near their people, you will have better success getting your cat to use a scratching post if you place it in the room where you spend most of your time.

Introduce your Somali to its scratching post at an early age and it soon will learn to restrict its clawing to the post. Many cats like to stretch and scratch after napping. When you witness this behavior, simply carry the cat to the post and move its paws in a scratching motion. Praise your Somali when it scratches the post. If necessary, rub some dried catnip on the post to entice the animal and to give the post a positive association. If the cat decides to try out your furniture, scold verbally by saying "No" in a loud, sharp tone. Or squirt a jet of clean water from a water pistol to startle the cat without harming it. But *never, never* strike your cat with your hand, with a folded newspaper, or with any other object. Such abusive action only makes the cat fearful of you. If the cat persists in scratching the couch arm, cover the problem area temporarily with a loosely-draped blanket, wrapping paper, plastic bubble wrap, or sheets of aluminum foil. Some owners claim that rubbing a sliced, raw onion on the unsuitable area acts as a deterrent. To discourage undesirable scratching habits, you must somehow make the inappropriate surfaces unattractive to the cat while offering a more appealing substitute (see pages 74 and 75 for more information on scratching behaviors and declawing).

A cat usually rejects a scratching post because it doesn't like the material. For example, your cat may prefer bare wood or tree bark to carpet; it may prefer a rougher, loose-weave fabric, such as burlap; or it may prefer a flat, horizontal surface to a vertical, upright post. For clues, notice the surfaces your cat likes to scratch in your home or yard, then apply your observations to the next scratching post you build or buy.

Cat toys: Somalis love to play, and they will entertain their owners for hours batting about a wad of paper or an empty spool of thread. You don't have to spend lots of money on toys. Be creative and make toys for your cat. A marble or gravel safely sealed in an empty, plastic film case makes a tantalizing rattler. Ping-pong balls, golf balls, tennis balls, paper grocery bags (avoid plastic bags because cats, like children, may suffocate in them), and a cardboard box with cut-out peep holes make inexpensive toys.

Whether you make it or buy it, carefully consider a toy's safety before you give it to your cat. Ideally, you want a sturdy toy that won't disintegrate after the first few swipes. Remove tied-on bells, plastic eyes, button noses, and dangling strings that your cat could

Interactive cat toys offer a great way to spend quality time with your Somali, but store them safely out of reach when not in use.

tear off and swallow or choke on during play. Never let your Somali play with small items that could be chewed or swallowed easily, such as buttons, hair pins, rubber bands, wire bread-wrapper ties, paper clips, cellophane, or candy wrappers. Also, avoid yarn balls, threaded spools, or string of any kind. Supervise all access to fishing-pole-style toys with feathers, sparklers, and tied-on lures that whirl through the

Window perches allow indoor cats to enjoy the natural world outside, but make sure window screens are sturdy and secure.

To avoid clawing problems, provide your Somali with a scratching post.

air. These interactive toys provide great exercise, but put them in a closet when you're not playing with your cat. Also, be careful of braided rugs or knitted afghans that might unravel if the cat plays with a loose end. Once a cat starts chewing and swallowing string or yarn, a considerable amount may amass in the digestive tract and cause life-threatening blockages or perforations. If you come home to find your cat with a piece of string hanging out of its mouth, do *not* pull on the string. You have no way of knowing how much string has been swallowed and how much already has wound its way into the intestinal tract. Seek veterinary help immediately. Surgery may be required to correct the condition.

Catnip: Pet stores offer an array of catnip mice, catnip sacks, and other scented toys. Catnip, a member of the mint family, is a perennial herb you can grow indoors or outdoors for your cat's entertainment. Some cats go wild

over it and will roll ecstatically in the dried leaves or with a scented toy. Afterward, they lie sprawled on their backs in a trancelike state, as if drunk, purring loudly and contentedly. The compound in the plant that causes this reaction is called *nepetalactone.* The effect wears off in a short time, and the herb is not thought to be addictive or harmful to domestic cats. However, not all cats care for catnip. A significant number lack the gene that makes them respond to the plant's intoxicating effects and show no marked reaction when exposed to it.

Most pet stores sell dried catnip or kits to grow your own at home. To make a catnip pillow, cut heavy-duty fabric in two squares, sew together on three sides wrong side out, turn right side out (seams will be inside sack), stuff dried catnip in open end and sew shut.

Window perches: These carpeted shelves that attach easily to windowsills give the indoor cat an eye to the outside world and help ease occasional bouts of boredom. Place a bird feeder or bird bath in view of the window, and your Somali will be entertained for hours, as if watching "cat TV." Giving your cat its own window rest lookout also helps train it to stay out of other window locations where you might not want it to lounge.

To prevent falls and escapes, make sure all window screens lock in place and are sturdy, tight, and secure enough to withstand the cat's weight if it lunges at a fluttering moth on the outside. Veterinarians treat enough injured cats that fall or jump from upper-story windows to give the condition a name—high-rise syndrome.

Hazards in the Home

Besides flimsy window screens, other hazards in the home include:
• uncovered sump pumps
• toilet lids left up (kittens can fall in and drown)

- household chemicals
- poisonous plants
- open trash bins
- open appliance doors
- open fires and electrical cords

To make your home cat-safe, do the same things you would do to make it child-safe:

- Screen fireplaces.
- Put detergents, solvents, mothballs, insect sprays, and other potentially dangerous substances high out of reach in securely closed cabinets.
- Since some Somalis become proficient at prying open cupboard doors, install locks or latches, if necessary.
- Remember, cats don't have to deliberately drink a household chemical to get poisoned by it. They can ingest wax, bleach, detergents, and other toxic chemicals simply by brushing against dirty containers or walking through spills, then licking the substance off their paws and fur. For this reason, use common sense and don't let your cat walk across wet paint, waxed floors, or disinfected counter tops until surfaces dry.
- Don't put out edible rodent and insect baits where your cat might get at them and be poisoned.
- In the bathroom, keep perfumes, cosmetics, nail polish removers, and all vitamins and medicines, including aspirin and acetaminophen (toxic to cats), tightly capped and put away. If knocked over or spilled, your cat may accidentally consume a harmful substance or be cut on shattered glass.
- Use covered trash cans in the bathroom, as well as in all other rooms, to prevent a curious cat from digging out potentially dangerous items, such as discarded razor blades, used dental floss (string), tossed-out pills, and broken glass.
- In the laundry room, keep washer and dryer doors shut, as these offer warm, dark, tempting places for cats to crawl in and sleep unseen. Before

Keep electrical cords unplugged when not in use, or cover them with carpeting, matting, or plastic piping.

you shut any appliance door, make sure your cat hasn't jumped in unnoticed. Likewise, in the kitchen, your Somali will be underfoot without fail whenever you open the refrigerator door. If accidentally shut inside, your cat could suffocate or suffer from cold exposure.

- Until your Somali learns to leave cords alone, tuck electrical and telephone cords out of reach under mats or carpets, tack them down or cover them with PVC piping. Coating cords with bitter apple, bitter lime (available in spray bottles at pet stores), raw onion juice, or tabasco sauce also helps discourage chewing. Chewing on electrical cords can result in burns and electric shock. If this happens, disconnect the current before touching the cat, or use a wooden broom handle to disengage the cat from the wire. Even if the cat appears to suffer only minor burns to the tongue and mouth, consult a veterinarian immediately. Complications can occur later, because electric shock sometimes alters normal lung and heart functions.

• Keep window and drapery cords tied up and out of reach, as a frolicking feline can become entangled and accidentally strangle itself.

• Dangling cords from a coffee pot or from an iron left sitting upright on the ironing board pose a tempting threat. A playful cat can pull an unattended hot appliance down on top of itself. The inquisitive Somali that leaps up on counters and stove tops when you're not looking can be burned accidentally by stepping on a hot burner or by sniffing a boiling saucepan or tea kettle. When in use, keep a close eye on hot appliances, just as you would if a small child were in the house. Unplug them when not in use.

• Remove or secure fragile ornaments and alcoholic beverage containers that an exploring cat might knock over and break.

• Put away pins, needles, and threads when not in use to prevent your Somali from accidentally swallowing them.

• Even some of your children's toys could pose potential dangers to a cat. For example, indoor basketball hoops over trash cans can trap a curious kitten in the netting, causing accidental strangulation.

• Outdoors, some lawn pesticides, weed killers, fungicides, and fertilizers pose hazards to pets that walk in treated grass, then lick the chemicals off their paws. If you allow your cat outside for supervised jaunts, read labels before using any lawn product. Many professional lawn services recommend keeping pets inside until after the next rain rinses chemicals off the grass and into the soil.

• Although cats can swim, swimming pools or fish ponds represent a significant hazard; they can drown from exhaustion if they fall in and can't find a way out. Kittens, especially, are at risk because they're too small to climb out without help. If you have a pool or pond in your yard, supervise your pets around it as carefully as you would watch your children.

• In the garage or driveway, wipe up and hose down antifreeze spills immediately. Ethylene glycol, the prime ingredient in traditional antifreeze, has a pleasant taste that attracts animals to drink. The substance is poisonous, and as little as half a teaspoon can kill an adult cat. New "safer antifreeze" products on the market contain propylene glycol, which is significantly less toxic than ethylene glycol. In fact, propylene glycol is used as a preservative in some foods, alcoholic beverages, cosmetics, and pharmaceuticals. Consider replacing your old antifreeze with a safer brand, and check under your car periodically to make sure no antifreeze or other fluids are leaking.

• In winter, cats allowed outside often crawl up under car hoods to sleep, because the engines stay warm for many hours after use. To alert sleeping cats, cautious people bang on the hood or blow the horn before starting the car. The fan blades and other engine parts can cause fatal injuries if an unsuspecting feline gets caught underneath, another good reason to keep your Somali safely indoors.

Hazardous Plants

Although carnivorous by nature, cats enjoy snacking on greenery, apparently because the added roughage aids in digestion. Unfortunately, cats often indulge this occasional craving by nibbling on decorative houseplants and ornamental shrubs. While many plants are harmless to cats, others are deadly. Ingestion can cause a wide range of symptoms, including mouth irritation, drooling, vomiting, diarrhea, hallucinations, convulsions, lethargy, and coma. If your cat displays any unusual behavior after chewing on a

Hazardous Plants

Amaryllis	Daphne	Jack-in-the-pulpit	Peyote
Asparagus fern	Datura	Jerusalem cherry	Philodendron
Azalea	Delphinium	Jimsonweed	Poinsettia
Belladonna	Dieffenbachia	Larkspur	Pokeweed
Bird of paradise	(Spotted dumb	Lily of the valley	Potato
Black locust	cane)	Lupin	Rhododendron
Caladium	Elephant ear	Marijuana	Rhubarb
Castor bean	Foxglove	Mistletoe	Skunk cabbage
Chinaberry	Fruit pits	Monkshood	Spider mum
Christmas cherry	Hemlock	Moonseed	Umbrella plant
Christmas rose	Henbane	Morning glory	Wild cherry
Chrysanthemum	Holly	Mushrooms	Wisteria
Clematis	Honeysuckle	Nightshade	Yew
Creeping Charlie	Hydrangea	Nutmeg	
Crown of thorns	Iris	Oleander	
Daffodil	Ivy	Periwinkle	

plant, consult a veterinarian immediately. Be prepared to induce vomiting if advised to do so (see Accidental Poisoning, page 59).

To make your house and yard cat-safe, avoid the common toxic plants listed above.

The list is only a partial one; therefore, if you are unsure about a particular plant's toxicity, call your veterinarian, poison control center, or local agricultural extension agent. Besides nibbling on the greenery, it's also quite natural for a cat to mistake the dirt-filled base of a large potted houseplant for a convenient litter box. Unless you like your plants fertilized in this manner, cover the dirt with decorative rock.

Introducing Your Somali to Other Pets

Once the house is made safe, you're ready to introduce your Somali to its new home. If you already have an adult cat or a dog, bringing a new kitten into their "territory" must be managed carefully. Before exposing any newcomer to your resident cat(s), have it checked by a veterinarian and tested for disease, especially feline leukemia virus (FeLV) and feline immune deficiency virus (FIV). While awaiting the test results, keep the new arrival isolated from other pets, in a separate room or in a pen. This also allows time for the "house smell" to settle on the newcomer, which often helps make the introductions less threatening. After a few days, remove the new cat from its separate quarters for awhile and let the resident pets go in and sniff the new scent. When the time seems right, allow the resident pets to see and sniff the newcomer, but supervise all contact for the first few weeks. Keep dogs on a leash during these first meetings so they won't chase and frighten the newcomer. Gradually increase the exposure until the pets seem to coexist peaceably.

If you have rabbits, guinea pigs, birds, or other small pets, it's possible to achieve harmony among the different species as long as you provide secure, separate living quarters for all and supervise any direct contact. Never leave adult cats alone with uncaged birds and small animals of prey. Cover aquariums with a hood, so cats won't be tempted to go fishing.

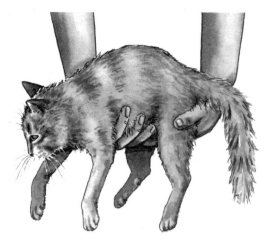

To pick up and hold a Somali properly, place one hand behind the front legs, support the rear legs with the other hand, . . .

Although it's usually easier to introduce a kitten, rather than a grown cat, into a home that already has a feline, don't be dismayed if it takes as long as a month for the animals to accept each other and settle down. Cats are territorial, and adding a newcomer means new boundaries must be set. In time, the tension usually disappears.

. . . and cradle the cat upright in your arms against your chest.

However, cats, like people, are individuals, and occasionally two simply may not like each other and may never adjust well. Many breeders will offer to buy back a kitten if things don't work out in the new home, and ideally, the sales contract should spell out the terms of a return agreement.

Introducing Your Somali to Children

Children find kittens irresistible, but they have to be taught how to handle them properly. Not only can a child injure a fragile kitten, but an animal that is frightened or annoyed by a child's unintentional roughness may defend itself by scratching or biting the child. To avoid such mishaps, teach your child early that pets are not animated toys. If the child pulls on a cat's tail or ears, remove his or her hand and indicate how to gently stroke the animal's fur. Supervise all physical contact, and explain to your child that loud screams and sudden movements may frighten the cat. Show your child where cats like to be stroked most—under the chin, behind the ears, and on the neck and back. Explain that some cats do not like to be stroked on their stomachs and rumps, while others will tolerate it from people they know well and trust. Teach your child how to properly pick up and hold a cat.

Picking Up a Cat

To pick up a cat, put one hand under the chest behind the forelegs and the other hand under the rump to support the rear legs and body. Cradle the cat in your arms against your chest. Your Somali will let you know when it wants down. Do not try to hold onto a struggling cat that wants to be put down. You will succeed only in making it dislike being held. Although mother cats carry their kittens by the scruff of the neck, this method can hurt an adult cat if not done properly and should be reserved for emergency restraint. Even then, care must be taken to fully support the cat's rear legs and body weight with the other hand. Letting it dangle can injure those neck and back muscles. Likewise, never lift a cat by its front paws.

Cats and Babies

Contrary to ridiculous "old wives' tales" you may have heard about cats sucking milk from infants' mouths and smothering them, cats and babies can coexist peaceably as long as you use some common-sense precautions. Don't allow your cat to have unsupervised access to an infant, not because there's any truth to the old wives' tales, but because screams, cries, or jerky movements made by the infant could frighten the cat and result in accidental scratching or biting. If necessary, install a screen door at the nursery entrance. Also, to keep cats out of the cradle or crib, consider buying a mesh crib tent. Baby supply stores sell these as well as cat nets that cover playpens and strollers.

Sometimes a cat may urinate on a baby's bedding or other items, "marking" them as part of its territory. Spaying and neutering tend to curb marking behaviors (see page 73 for more information on territorial marking). To reduce accidental scratches, trim your cat's claws regularly. And keep your cat in good health and free of parasites to reduce any risk of disease transmission to your child.

Toxoplasmosis deserves a mention here, because it's one of those scary reasons well-meaning people bring up to convince mothers-to-be that their cats must go before a new baby comes. Before you do anything so drastic, get the facts first from your obstetrician and veterinarian, if you're planning to have a baby. Tests are available to detect the disease, which is caused by a protozoan. If a preg-

Some decorative plants in your home and yard may be harmful to your Somali.

nant woman is exposed to it, birth defects can occur. Cats get the disease by eating infected birds, rodents, or raw meat. Then they shed the eggs in their feces. Humans can get it by handling soil or litter contaminated by the feces of an infected cat; however, the majority of cases result from eating undercooked meat.

If your Somali never roams outdoors, never hunts and never eats anything except pre-packaged pet food, the chances of it having the disease are nearly nonexistent. To avoid exposure, cook meats thoroughly and never feed your cat raw or undercooked meat. If you become pregnant, wear gloves when gardening and when cleaning the litter box. Better yet, delegate the latter chore to someone else. If you know the facts and observe

A cat flap allows your Somali safe access to an outdoor exercise run or a screened porch.

sensible precautions, there's no need whatsoever to get rid of your cat if you're going to have a baby.

Note: As a general health precaution, keep indoor litter boxes and pet feeding bowls out of a crawling child's range. And cover children's sandboxes when not in use, so that free-roaming cats won't mistake them for giant, outdoor litter boxes.

Holiday Hazards

Accidental poisonings are a particular hazard around the Christmas holidays because many people decorate with poinsettia, holly berries, and mistletoe, all of which are toxic to cats. Chocolate also is toxic to cats, so don't leave desserts and candy dishes exposed where your Somali might sample the goodies when you're not looking.

To prevent a curious, climbing cat from toppling the Christmas tree, anchor it to the wall or ceiling by tying it to a hook. Use unbreakable ornaments. Baubles, bells, and branches on Christmas trees present an irresistible temptation to playful paws. Somalis especially love to play with and eat the tinsel that dangles so alluringly from decorated trees. While not toxic, the

string-like foil can cause serious intestinal obstructions or perforations when swallowed. The same is true of angel hair, edible ornaments, and small plastic beads or berries.

In addition, aspirin and some commercial chemicals used as preservatives in Christmas tree water can be lethal to cats that might drink from the tree base. Either avoid these chemicals, as well as others used for decoration, such as artificial snow, or keep cats out of the decorated room when you aren't present to supervise. Keep electrical cords on holiday decorations covered or out of reach, and unplug the Christmas tree lights when not in use.

Sometimes, people pose the greatest hazard to pets at holiday time. If your party guests tend to drink too much, put your cat away in a quiet, safe part of the house while you entertain. This way, no one will accidentally step on or stumble over your cat or be tempted to offer it potentially toxic party treats, such as alcohol.

Halloween is a dangerous time for cats allowed outdoors, especially black ones, because some fall victim to vicious pranks. But holiday or not, some people dislike cats so much that they may employ deadly means to keep them out of their flower gardens and trash cans, which is reason enough to keep your cat safely indoors at all times.

Indoor Versus Outdoor Cats

Some people insist on letting their cats roam freely because they believe that depriving cats of their outdoor freedom is cruel. Most humane educators disagree, for many good reasons. Cats kept indoors live longer, healthier lives because they are less likely to be exposed to diseases, plagued by parasites, hit by cars, attacked by dogs, bitten by wild animals, caught in wild animal traps, poisoned by pesticides, and harmed by cruel people. By keeping your Somali indoors, you will have fewer veterinary bills related to injuries from cat fights and similar mishaps. In addition, you will have peace of mind, knowing that your well-kept indoor cat has little chance of contracting a disease or parasite that could be transmitted to you or your family. As long as you provide love and attention, your Somali will be quite happy and well-adjusted living indoors. If you feel your Somali must experience the outdoors, supervise outings in the yard, build an outdoor exercise run, or install a cat flap that provides safe access to a screened-in porch. You also can teach your Somali to walk on a leash, but never tie a cat outdoors unattended; that's dangerous.

Leash Training

With patience and perseverance, your Somali can be taught to tolerate a leash; just don't expect your cat to "heel" with precision by your side the way a trained dog does. Some cats take to walking on a leash better than others. Somalis are smart and learn tricks quickly; however, much depends on individual temperament. To begin, select an adjustable nylon or leather cat harness and a lightweight leash. Most pet supply stores and catalogs market harnesses designed specifically to restrain cats so that they can't slip free and escape. Do *not* use a choker collar or a dog harness on a cat.

First, accustom the cat to the harness by putting it on when you're home to supervise. Let the cat drag the leash freely behind it, but don't leave the cat unattended while doing this, because it might get entangled or accidentally hang itself. When the cat seems used to wearing the equipment, pick up the leash and, using a pull toy for enticement, gently coax it along for a short distance. Praise your cat lavishly when it takes a few steps in the desired direction. Then, when your Somali walks

Somalis learn quickly and many can be trained to walk on a harness and leash.

comfortably with you on a leash inside the house, take it outside for short walks in a quiet area. Until your cat adjusts to unfamiliar sights and sounds outdoors, take along a pet carrier. Then, if something frightens the cat and causes it to struggle on the leash, simply pop it in the carrier for safety.

Pet Identification

Cats allowed outdoors sometimes stray too far from home and then can't find their way back. Even cats kept indoors occasionally escape and get lost in unfamiliar territory. For these reasons, and because some people steal pets for sale to research laboratories, your cat is safer if it wears some sort of identification.

Tattooing: While tattooing won't prevent your cat from being lost or stolen, a permanent ID may enhance

Introducing a kitten to an adult cat can be accomplished with patience, care, and supervision. (Photo courtesy of American Greetings Corporation, © AGC, Inc.)

its chances of recovery. Many laboratories will not buy a tattooed animal, and most shelters look for tattoos. A painless procedure provided by many veterinarians, tattooing involves inking the owner's Social Security number or a special code on the rear inner thigh. For best results, keep the area shaved and register the tattoo with a nationwide pet protection service that has a 24-hour hotline for tracing the number and finding the owner, no matter where the cat is found (see Useful Addresses and Literature, page 106).

Collars and tags: These can be lost or removed, but they are better than nothing. A cat collar needs to have a stretch elastic or a breakaway section, so the animal can escape without choking if the collar catches on some object.

Like collars, ear tags embedded in the ear like a tiny earring are better than no ID at all, but they, too, can be cut off, ear and all, by desperate, unscrupulous pet thieves.

Microchips: Shelters in some areas use microchip technology to reunite lost pets with their owners. With this ID system, a veterinarian injects a tiny microchip under the skin between the cat's shoulder blades. The chip reflects radio waves emitted by a hand-held scanner that reads the chip's code number. The owner registers the code number in a computer database for tracking. Ask your veterinarian if this system is available in your area.

Feeding Your Somali

Life-Cycle Nutrition

Cats, like people, are what they eat. However, the relative term, "good nutrition," depends largely on your cat's age, activity level, and current state of health. Research has shown that certain nutrients consumed at too high or too low levels during early life stages may contribute to health problems in later life. This knowledge led to a departure from the old "womb-to-tomb" practice of feeding cats one food their entire lives, and ushered in a new era of "life-cycle nutrition." Today, life-cycle formulas scientifically tailored to meet a cat's nutritional needs during different stages of its life compete for grocery store shelf space. But with so many specialty pet foods to choose from—reduced-calorie diets, special-care formulas, low-magnesium products—the important thing to remember is that no one perfect pet food exists for every cat and for every owner.

Although pet food labels provide helpful information, choosing a cat food solely by label contents or by brand name is unwise. Instead, base your selection on how well your Somali performs and maintains its overall condition on a particular food. Start with foods your breeder or veterinarian recommends. Then, during annual checkups, your veterinarian can assess your Somali's condition as it grows and matures and advise you about dietary changes and requirements.

Make any changes to your Somali's diet gradually, over a period of a week or two. Start the change by giving your Somali small portions of the new food mixed with its present food. Gradually increase the amount of new food as you decrease the amount of old food until the replacement is complete.

Kitten Feeding

For its first full year, your Somali kitten needs more high-quality protein for growth than it will require in adulthood. Many kitten formulas come in smaller pellets that make it easier for tiny kitten mouths to chew. At least 30 to 40 percent of a kitten's diet should be protein. Select a kitten or feline growth formula designed to meet this extra need and follow the feeding guidelines. Kittens need to be fed more often and in smaller quantities than adult cats. Generally, newly weaned kittens require three or four feedings a day. At six months, reduce feedings to twice a day.

Adult Feeding

Moderately active adult cats need enough nutrients, fiber, and protein to satisfy their appetites, yet prevent them from getting fat, so put them on a suitable adult maintenance diet. Pregnant cats need more calories and high-quality protein because of the extra demand placed on their bodies. To aid in fetal development and milk production, select a feline growth and reproduction formula for breeding females during gestation and lactation. Older, less active cats generally need fewer calories and less salt, so with your veterinarian's advice, choose a "senior" or "light" diet plan for them.

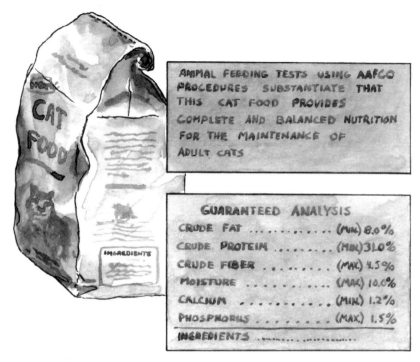

ANIMAL FEEDING TESTS USING AAFCO PROCEDURES SUBSTANTIATE THAT THIS CAT FOOD PROVIDES COMPLETE AND BALANCED NUTRITION FOR THE MAINTENANCE OF ADULT CATS

GUARANTEED ANALYSIS

CRUDE FAT	(MIN)	8.0%
CRUDE PROTEIN	(MIN)	31.0%
CRUDE FIBER	(MAX)	4.5%
MOISTURE	(MAX)	10.0%
CALCIUM	(MIN)	1.2%
PHOSPHORUS	(MAX)	1.5%

INGREDIENTS ....

If a product's statement of nutritional adequacy says "complete and balanced for mainte-nance of the adult cat," the food would not be satisfactory for kittens or pregnant or nursing queens. The guaranteed analysis gives approximate nutrient percentages based on the total material in the can or package, water and all. The ingredients list discloses the food's contents in decreasing order by weight.

Dry, Soft-Dry Foods Versus Canned

Commercial pet foods come in three types: dry, semimoist (soft-dry), and canned. Generally, dry foods are less expensive and more convenient.

Dry foods can be left all day in a bowl for cats to nibble at will, whereas canned foods spoil if left out too long. In addition to their convenience, dry foods help maintain better dental health, because the hard chewing action scours the teeth and gums. Because Somalis are prone to gingivitis (gum inflammation), dry foods are a healthful choice for them. Dry foods usually con-tain more cereals, while canned foods have more protein and fat, making them

generally more palatable to the cat. To enhance flavor, manufacturers often spray dry foods with liquid meat digests. At one time, it was thought that nibbling on dry foods throughout the day predisposed cats to feline urologic syndrome (FUS) by allowing the urine pH to become too alkaline. This theory is now outdated, because most major cat food brands have been reformulated to maintain urine pH levels within nor-mal acidic ranges.

Soft-dry nuggets or semimoist foods attempt to combine some bene-fits of the dry and canned forms, mak-ing them more attractive to the human consumer. Like dry rations, semimoist nuggets can be left out and fed free-choice without spoiling, and they do not have as much of an odor as canned foods. Unlike dry foods, semi-moist products are too soft to help reduce dental tartar. Originally, these products contained a preservative called propylene glycol. When this preservative was implicated in causing red blood cell damage, responsible cat food manufacturers removed it from their products. Now, most product labels, except some treats, should no longer list it as an ingredient.

Canned foods contain more moisture than either dry or semimoist foods, making them a better choice for cats needing greater water intake. Feed canned products twice daily, or according to the label instructions, and remove the leftovers as soon as the cat finishes eating. Finicky eaters seem to like canned food better, although many will not touch it after it has been refrigerated. Most cats prefer their food at room temperature.

With so many choices available, it's easy to find a good product that your Somali enjoys and that is convenient for you to serve. To provide variety and appetite appeal, select two or three high-quality products your Somali seems to like and use them inter-changeably. Choose products guaranteed on the label to provide "complete and balanced nutrition" for your Somali's current life cycle—kitten, adult, pregnant, and nursing, etc.

Popular Versus Premium Brands

Cat foods are marketed according to generic, popular (supermarket brands), and premium brands. While the less expensive generic foods often tend to be lower in quality, that's not always true. Sometimes it's cheaper for a manufacturer to simply stick a generic label on a popular brand name without changing the formula. The more expensive premium brands are sold primarily

The dry weight or dry matter of a food is that portion that would be left over if all of the water were subtracted. For example, if the label says the moisture content is 78 percent, then the dry matter is 22 percent. Converting percentages to a dry matter basis is the best way to accurately compare contents of canned foods with dry or semi-moist foods.

through pet stores and veterinarians' offices. Other than price, supermarket brands and premium brands have one crucial difference. Premium foods remain stable in their makeup, whereas supermarket brands are more likely to change recipe ingredients according to the current market cost and availability of those ingredients. That's why an owner who always feeds the same popular brand may notice a change in the cat's stool volume or coat condition from time to time.

Premium brands may cost more, but their stable mixtures generally contain higher-quality ingredients. That's why their formulas usually promote a shinier hair coat, greater digestibility, and lower stool volume. The product research behind premium brands is often more substantial, as well.

Prescription diets also are available through veterinarians for cats with special needs due to heart disease, kidney disease, intestinal disorders, obesity, or other health problems. While most special diets come in dry

Your Somali kitten needs a high-protein kitten formula for its first full year.

(too high), providing favorable conditions for the crystals to form in the urinary tract. Magnesium content remains a secondary concern, enough to warrant restricting dietary levels when managing FUS. Reflecting this knowledge, specialty foods proliferate the market bearing label claims of "low magnesium," "reduces urinary pH," or "helps maintain urinary tract health." Beyond these permissible statements, cat food manufacturers cannot claim that their products treat or prevent FUS, or any disease, without approval from the Food and Drug Administration, because to do so would be touting the diet as a drug. These special diets, as well as many regular cat foods now on the market, contain enough acidifying ingredients to help keep urine pH within safely acidic ranges. An acid urine helps dissolve struvite crystals or prevents them from forming in the first place.

In the last 10 years, researchers have noted a decrease in struvite stones along with an increase in similar stones composed of calcium oxalate. No doubt, the recomposition of commercial diets fed to cats brought about both changes, at least in part. While studies clearly suggest that restricting magnesium and maintaining a slightly acidic urine may help prevent struvite-related urethral obstructions, such a diet is not a cure-all for *all* cats, particularly if it has the potential to cause other problems. What all this really means is that, while perhaps not perfect, most cat foods are better than they used to be, due to research. And while the link between diet and urinary tract disease remains under investigation, the best advice is to consult your veterinarian before starting your cat on any special diet.

or canned form, at least one for recurrent gastrointestinal problems is available in soft-dry nuggets.

Diet and Urinary Tract Health

Over the years, numerous dietary constituents have been blamed in the formation of struvite crystals that can plug the urethra in FUS, a potentially life-threatening disease. (**Note:** Some veterinarians refer to FUS as LUTD, or lower urinary tract disease, an umbrella term used to describe all disorders of the lower urinary tract.) The suspect list includes ash, magnesium, phosphorous, calcium, and ingredients that influence the body's acid-base balance, among others. As each was incriminated, major cat food manufacturers promptly reformulated their foods to reflect current scientific opinion.

Current findings suggest that the *overall* mineral composition of cat food, rather than an excess of any single ingredient, determines whether the urine pH balance becomes too alkaline

Deciphering a Cat Food Label

Complete and Balanced: Pet food companies are required by law to

Like most cats, Somalis like to relax and groom themselves after a satisfying meal.

supply certain nutritional information on their labels. Only snack foods and treats are exempt. To show their products meet nutritional guidelines outlined by the Association of American Feed Control Officials (AAFCO), pet food manufacturers often conduct chemical analyses and/or feeding trials. Feeding trials offer more assurance that food is adequately nutritious, because the product has been test fed to cats for a period of time under AAFCO protocols. Any product that has undergone feeding trials usually says so on the package. Look for the company's statement of nutritional adequacy, which should say something similar to: *"Animal feeding tests using AAFCO procedures substantiate that [this brand name] provides complete and balanced nutrition for the maintenance of adult cats."*

Guaranteed Analysis: Labels can be misleading. The required "guaranteed analysis," listing content percentages, must contain statements on the label only about whether minimum or maximum amounts were met, but

actual concentrations of specific nutrients need not be listed. The problem with not knowing how much a product exceeds the minimum requirement for a certain nutrient, such as protein, is that sometimes too much can be just as bad as too little, depending on the cat's age and condition. Thus, while foods formulated for "all life stages of cats" are designed to meet normal nutritional needs from kittenhood through seniorhood, some individuals, particularly those predisposed to certain health problems, may get far more of certain nutrients than they need.

Ingredients List: Ingredients are supposed to be listed in descending order of predominance by weight; however, this, too, may be misleading. For example, meat may be listed first, leading the consumer to believe the product contains mostly meat, when in reality, the summation of separately listed grains and cereals makes plant material the predominant ingredient. Some labeling terms are strictly regulated, while others are not. For example, the title wording of "Chicken for

Cats," "Chicken Platter," "Chicken Entree," etc., have different meanings in terms of the percentage of chicken contained in the product. A good way to check specific ingredient amounts is simply to call the manufacturer's number on the package and ask for the data. Many companies have consulting veterinarians and/or nutritionists, and you can judge for yourself how willing and able they seem to be to answer your questions. The manufacturer's reputation can offer some assurance that correct product standards are met and maintained.

Dry Weight Analysis: Because label percentages are based on the entire food formula—water and all—one must standardize the base of comparison when reading labels of different types of cat foods. This is done by calculating the "dry weight," the food content that would be left if all of the water were removed. First, determine the percentages of moisture and dry matter in the food. The guaranteed analysis already contains part of this information. If the label says the moisture content is 78 percent, subtract that figure from 100 percent (total food formula) to calculate the dry matter. In this case, the dry matter in the food is 22 percent.

Once you've calculated the dry matter, you can do a dry weight analysis for each nutrient in the food, based on the label guarantees. The formula for this is simple:

$$\frac{\% \text{ Nutrient}}{\% \text{ Dry Matter}}$$

For example, we've already determined that the dry matter is 22 percent; now we want to know how much of that matter is protein. The guaranteed analysis on the label says the food contains a minimum of 10 percent crude protein. (**Note:** The word "crude" means the maximum or minimum

amount was determined by laboratory assay and not by feeding tests.) That 10 percent figure is based on the food's total formula, including moisture content. However, on a dry matter basis, the protein content is:

$$\frac{10\%}{22\%} = 45\%$$

To support normal growth and reproduction, AAFCO recommends that at least 30 percent of a cat's diet be protein. For maintenance of adult cats, protein content should be at least 26 percent. These are recommended *minimum* amounts, based on dry matter, that foods should contain. In the above example, the label guarantees the product to be no less than 45 percent protein (dry weight basis), but it doesn't tell whether the actual protein content exceeds that stated minimum. This information might be important if, for example, your cat requires a protein-reduced diet.

Although the dry weight analysis is a good way to compare nutrient percentages in different types of foods, it's not an exact measurement of daily nutrient intake. Remember, label guarantees are expressed either in minimum (not *less* than) or maximum (not *more* than) percentages, but not in actual amounts. If you're concerned about feeding too much or too little of a certain ingredient, consult your veterinarian. He can best judge your Somali's individual nutritional needs.

How Much and When to Feed

As a guide to daily rations, follow the feeding instructions on the package. Remember, however, that the recommended amounts are estimates based on feeding trials. The amount of food your Somali requires each day will vary with its age, weight, and activity level. Adjust the rations as necessary to maintain optimum body weight and condition. Generally speaking, a cat is at its optimum weight when you cannot see the ribs, but you can feel them without probing through thick layers of fat. Here again, your veterinarian can best judge your Somali's overall condition and dietary requirements.

Most adult cats thrive on two meals a day—morning and evening. Others do well on a canned food breakfast, combined with ample dry food left out for free-choice nibbling. Whatever routine you prefer, feed your Somali at the same time and in the same place each day. Keep food bowls clean.

Milk and Water

Keep fresh water in a clean bowl available for your Somali at all times. Cats can concentrate their urine and conserve water when necessary; however, like most other mammals, they can survive only a number of days without water before suffering severe metabolic distress.

Milk is a food and not a substitute for water. Although useful as a supplement for newly weaned kittens, milk as a staple cat food is incomplete and not a balanced diet. As a supplement for growing kittens, experts usually recommend a canned kitten formula or a half-and-half mixture of evaporated milk and water instead of homogenized cow's milk. Some adult cats, like some people, develop a lactose intolerance to milk and will get diarrhea if they drink it.

The Folly of Homemade Diets

To remain healthy, cats, being obligate carnivores by nature, need protein from animal sources. They cannot adapt safely to a vegetarian diet. Nor can they thrive solely on "people food." Their nutritional needs are quite specific and significantly different from those of humans, dogs, and other mammals; therefore, constructing a balanced meal for a cat from scratch is a chore best left to the experts.

100% − 78% = 22%

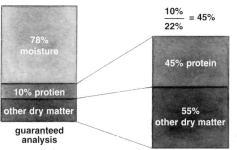

$$\frac{10\%}{22\%} = 45\%$$

Having determined the dry matter content of a food, you may calculate a dry weight analysis for each nutrient. For example, a canned food shows label guarantees of 10 percent protein and 78 percent water. By dry weight analysis, however, the protein is 10 percent divided by 22 percent (dry matter), which equals 45 percent protein.

Reputable pet food manufacturers budget substantial amounts of money for research to back claims that their products are nutritionally "complete and balanced." Without expert guidance, the home-based chef cannot guarantee an adequate mix of proteins, carbohydrates, fats, vitamins, minerals, and amino acids essential to the feline diet.

One amino acid in particular, taurine, is an indispensable additive, because cats cannot manufacture this ingredient on their own. If its food is taurine deficient, a cat could develop eye disorders or cardiomyopathy (heart muscle disease). Research into the cause of these disorders prompted responsible pet food manufacturers to increase the amount of taurine added to their feline products.

Nutritional additives in commercial pet foods often include vitamin supplements, such as A, D, E, and B-complex, and minerals, such as calcium, phosphorus, magnesium, potassium, salt, iron and zinc, among others. The feline diet requires a delicate balance of these ingredients to maintain proper body functions and cell growth. Too much or too little can be harmful.

Non-nutritional additives include preservatives and artificial colors approved by the Food and Drug Administration. Preservatives extend a product's shelf life and prevent fat rancidity, while artificial colors benefit only the human consumer by making a product's appearance more attractive. Home cooking should be attempted only in rare situations when a cat is suspected of being allergic to one of these additives or to other common ingredients in commercially prepared foods. Even then, the ingredients list in any homemade feline diet requires close veterinary supervision.

Obesity

Obesity is probably the most common nutritional disorder among pets in the United States. Fortunately, Somalis, active and playful by nature, are not as predisposed to this problem as some other breeds. As in humans, obesity in cats is a serious health risk because the extra weight puts a strain on all organ systems and contributes to a shortened life span. Also like humans, cats become fat for the same reasons—too many calories and too little exercise. While many cats with free access to food self-regulate their consumption appropriately, others overeat out of boredom. Owners sometimes contribute to the problem by offering too many gourmet treats between meals. In general, a cat is too fat if you cannot feel its ribs. Also, a fat cat's abdomen often becomes pendulous, and it may develop bulges of fat around the neck, face, and hips. Some

overweight cases are caused by feeding cats together, which encourages competition. In addition, many cats tend to gain weight as they grow older, because they become less active and need fewer calories. Weight gain and weight loss can be symptoms of serious underlying medical conditions, such as diabetes, thyroid disorders, and kidney disease; therefore, a veterinary examination is in order before you attempt to put your cat on any special diet.

Weight-Loss Diets

When putting a cat on a weight-loss diet, avoid a sudden and drastic reduction in calories. Gradual dietary changes, accomplished in about a week or 10 days, are less likely to cause stress reactions or aggressive behaviors. If switching to a reduced-calorie formula, do so by mixing increasing amounts of the new food with the old food, until the changeover is complete. Your veterinarian can recommend the best weight-reduction diets. These formulas are nutritionally balanced but lower in calories to produce weight loss without creating other deficiencies. They are also higher in fiber to promote a feeling of fullness. If you have more than one cat, you may have to feed the one on a special diet separately.

Foods to Avoid

Dog foods are for dogs. Cat foods are for cats. Be aware of the following:
• Do not feed your Somali dog food, because dog chow does not contain nearly enough protein or taurine to promote good health in cats. If you have a dog and a cat, provide each with its correct food, and feed them in separate locations if they steal each other's food. Also, vitamin and mineral supplements, unless prescribed by a veterinarian, are not necessary when you feed your Somali a complete and

nutritionally balanced commercial cat food. Pet food manufacturers add vitamins and minerals to their formulas to supplement and/or provide nutrients in addition to those contained in the primary ingredients.

• Table scraps do not provide a balanced diet, although they are okay as occasional treats. (Some owners report that their Somalis acquire an unusual liking for certain human foods, such as breads, fruits, and vegetables, so you may want to keep these products out of reach.) Garbage is garbage, however, so do not feed your Somali any scraps that you would not eat.

• Do not feed bones, as these may splinter and lodge in your cat's throat or puncture parts of the digestive tract.

• Keep trash cans tightly covered so your Somali cannot get into the garbage and ingest something potentially harmful, such as chicken bones or spoiled food.

• Do not feed raw meats, raw fish, raw liver, or raw egg whites. Meat alone is not a balanced meal and, if served raw, may contain parasites, including the organism that causes toxoplasmosis. Raw fish can cause a thiamine deficiency, and raw liver, if fed daily in large quantities, can cause vitamin A toxicity. Raw egg whites have an enzyme that can interfere with vitamin biotin absorption. An occasional egg yolk is okay, as long as it is cooked.

• Chocolate is toxic to cats and dogs, so keep candies, desserts, and baking chocolate covered and out of reach.

• Alcohol is toxic to cats, even in small amounts. Some unenlightened people think it's funny to let their cat

Despite their voracious appetites, Somalis generally stay fit and trim, like this one, because they are so active and playful.

lap up a little beer, then watch it stagger in drunken circles. This practice is cruel, dangerous, and sometimes deadly, as is deliberately blowing smoke from a cigarette or illegal substance into an animal's nostrils. A cat's smaller body mass cannot adequately absorb the toxic effects; therefore, just a little "hair of the dog" can affect an animal's breathing, cause shock, and lead to death.

Keeping Your Somali Healthy

The Veterinarian

Selecting a veterinarian for your Somali is one of the most important decisions you will make as a cat owner. Whether you choose someone in general veterinary practice or someone who treats cats exclusively, make sure you feel at ease with the way that person deals with you and your cat:
• Does he or she take time to answer your questions?
• Does he or she thoroughly explain procedures and findings?
• Does he or she show you how to give medications?
• Does the clinic offer additional services, such as grooming and boarding, that you might need?

Establish a good rapport with your veterinarian and his or her staff, because their professional guidance will be a valuable asset to your ongoing education as a pet owner. Keep the clinic's emergency number handy, in case your Somali becomes ill or injured.

When Something Is Wrong

Often, the first clue that something is wrong is a change in your cat's normal eating habits. Whether it shows a marked increase or decrease in appetite or stops eating altogether, regard any sudden and persistent change in behavior with suspicion. Likewise, if your Somali seems to be losing weight, drinking more water than normal, vomiting frequently, experiencing diarrhea, straining to urinate, or urinating more often, see your veterinarian. Other troublesome indications include coughing, sneezing, bleeding, staggering, swellings, panting, lethargy, lameness, coat changes, nasal discharge, bloody urine, bloody stool, crouching in a hunched-up position, hiding in unusual places, and difficulty breathing. The list is by no means exhaustive. Because cats often seek seclusion when sick or in pain, do not let your Somali go outdoors if you suspect something is wrong.

Check-ups and Vaccinations

The cost of treating a single illness can quickly exceed the total amount you spend on annual physical examinations and yearly booster shots throughout your Somali's lifetime. For this reason preventive health care makes good economic sense. Even

Frequent sneezing and sniffling may indicate a serious respiratory infection that warrants a visit to the veterinarian.

disease is extremely contagious, especially in kittens. Again, the best defense is vaccination.

Feline Panleukopenia Virus (FPV)

Sometimes called feline infectious enteritis, feline parvovirus and feline distemper, FPV bears no relation to the virus that causes distemper in dogs. The disease is destructive, highly contagious, and often fatal. Fortunately, it is less common than it once was, thanks, no doubt, to effective vaccines. Without early detection and treatment, the infected cat becomes desperately ill. Onset occurs four to six days after exposure, and early signs may include loss of appetite, depression, fever, and vomiting yellow bile. Because the virus often attacks the lining of the small intestine, a sick cat may have a painful abdomen and may cry out pitifully if touched. It may crouch in a stiff, hunched-up manner over its water bowl, as if wanting to drink but unable to. A lowered white blood cell count (leukopenia) confirms the diagnosis and gives the disease its name.

Feline Leukemia Virus (FeLV)

First discovered in 1964, FeLV is a retrovirus that suppresses the bone marrow and the immune system, rendering the cat vulnerable to various cancers, such as leukemia, and other secondary ailments. Symptoms vary but generally include weight loss, anemia, poor appetite, lethargy, and recurring infections. An infected cat can appear healthy for years before succumbing to an FeLV-related illness, but testing is available to determine FeLV status. The first FeLV vaccine took about 20 years to develop. Immunity is initiated with two injections spaced about a month apart, followed by annual boosters. Recent research has raised concerns about a low incidence of tumors (fibrosarcomas) developing at the injec-

Healthy, happy Somalis retain their desire to play well into adulthood. One youngster here seems about to engage in a game of "chase the tail."

tion sites of FeLV (and rabies) vaccines. While not caused by the vaccines directly, the tumors appear to result from a profound localized inflammation some cats experience, perhaps in reaction to aluminum compounds used in the vaccine suspension. For this reason, not all veterinarians recommend FeLV vaccination for *all* cats. Some recommend it only for cats at risk of contracting the disease, so be sure to discuss this with your veterinarian so you can make an informed choice. FeLV is the leading infectious cause of death in cats, and if your Somali gets it, there is no cure. Keep in mind that tumor development is extremely rare—about 10 to 12 cases for every 100,000 FeLV (or rabies) vaccines given. Unvaccinated cats face a far greater risk of developing fatal disease if exposed to the virus.

53

Cats allowed outdoors have the highest risk of FeLV exposure and certainly should be vaccinated. Others at risk include those living in multicat households and those exposed to outdoor cats, whether through direct contact or through screened windows. To be safe, any cat that comes into contact with other cats through breeding programs, at boarding kennels, or at cat shows needs protection against FeLV. Breeding toms and queens should be tested and certified free of the virus. Ideally, kittens should be tested before vaccination to rule out disease, because they can acquire the virus from an infected mother through the placenta or through the breast milk. If FeLV-positive, vaccination won't harm them, but it probably won't help. Because the disease passes from cat to cat through bite wounds and prolonged casual contact, all FeLV-positive cats should be kept indoors and isolated from FeLV-negative cats, even vaccinated ones. There is no evidence that FeLV is capable of causing disease in people.

Rabies

One of few feline ailments transmissible to humans, rabies occurs in nearly all warm-blooded animals. Skunks, foxes, raccoons, cats, and dogs account for most sporadic outbreaks. The fatal virus passes from an infected animal's saliva through a bite, open wound, or scrape. People bitten by a rabid animal must undergo a series of injections in order to save their lives.

Once inside the body, the virus travels to the brain, where it produces two characteristic forms: furious and paralytic, or "dumb," rabies. In the furious phase, cats exhibit personality changes that progress from subtle to severe. Normally affectionate and sociable cats may withdraw and hide. In a few days, they become irritable and dangerously aggressive. Animals in this "mad dog" stage often act frenzied and deranged and will attack viciously without provocation. In the dumb phase, paralysis overtakes the body, starting with the face, jaw, and throat muscles. Unable to swallow its own saliva, the animal drools or "foams at the mouth." Eventually, the rear legs give way, and the cat can no longer stand or walk. Death soon follows.

Fortunately, regular vaccination easily prevents this dreadful disease. Because of the threat to human health, most localities have laws requiring immunization of dogs and cats. To guarantee a certain immunity level, the first rabies shot requires a booster one year later. Thereafter, some regions permit boosters that last for three years. Without question, all outdoor cats should be immunized against rabies because of their potential exposure to infected animals, wild or domestic. Even if your Somali stays indoors, keep its rabies vaccinations current in case it bites someone or escapes to the outdoors. If your cat bites someone, you will need legal proof of immunization from your veterinarian.

Feline Infectious Peritonitis (FIP)

This potentially fatal illness is caused by a coronavirus that spurs an inflammatory reaction in the blood vessels and body tissues. The disease strikes primarily younger and older cats and those debilitated by other illnesses, such as feline leukemia virus. Common signs include fever, lethargy, appetite and weight loss, and an overall unthrifty appearance. FIP takes two forms, wet or dry. The wet form involves fluid buildup in the abdomen and chest. The cat exhibits labored breathing, extreme depression, and a swollen belly. The dry form progresses more slowly and affects many organs, including the liver, kidneys, pancreas, brain, and eyes. Because symptoms are often vague, this form is more difficult to diagnose. The first FIP vaccine became available in 1991 and is given through nose drops. Most veterinarians recommend it only if the exposure threat is high. The disease poses a greater hazard in catteries and multi-cat households, so discuss this vaccine option with your veterinarian.

Feline Immunodeficiency Virus (FIV)

Discovered in 1987, FIV is a retrovirus in the same family as FeLV and human immunodeficiency virus (HIV), the virus that causes AIDS. Although FIV is sometimes called "feline AIDS," it is important to understand that humans *cannot* catch this disease from cats. FIV is a species-specific virus, meaning that it infects only cats and is not transmissible to humans or to other animal species. The disease appears to be transmitted among cats mainly through bites. Because they often engage in territorial fighting, free-roaming males have the highest risk of contracting FIV. Cats kept indoors have the least risk. A test confirms a cat's FIV status, although no cure and no approved vaccines currently exist. Once contracted, the disease persists for life, although a cat may remain healthy for months or years before its immune system weakens enough to allow secondary infections to take hold. Symptoms vary but usually include lethargy, weight loss, gum disease, and chronic infections. The best prevention to date includes keeping your Somali indoors, thereby avoiding contact with potentially infected cats. Have new cats coming into your household tested for FIV (and FeLV) before introducing them to your Somali.

Renal Amyloidosis (RA)

Because Abyssinians appear to be slightly more susceptible to this rare but fatal kidney disorder than some other breeds, their sister breed, the Somali, also is affected. The disease, which is thought to be inherited, gets its name from a substance called amyloid that is deposited in the cat's kidneys, disrupting normal function. Death from kidney failure typically occurs between one and five years after onset. Symptoms include a poor hair coat, weight loss, decreased appetite, and increased thirst and urination. Although most Somalis do not develop this disorder, you certainly should ask a breeder if RA has shown up in the bloodlines before you buy a kitten. While some breeders guarantee their cats to be free of genetic defects, many do not, simply because of the unpredictable factors involved.

Lower Urinary Tract Disease (LUTD)

The urinary tract collects and disposes of urine through the bladder and a tube called the urethra. In female cats, the urethra is short and wide, whereas, in males, this opening, through which urine passes, is longer and more narrow. For this

Straining to urinate or any change in normal litter box habits may mean that your Somali has a lower urinary tract disorder that needs immediate veterinary treatment.

Excessive scratching may indicate fleas or an allergy. To inspect for fleas, rub your hand against the fur and look for black specks of "flea dirt" next to the skin.

within a short time from the backup pressure. As a result, toxic wastes build up in the blood, leading to death. With prompt medical treatment, most cats recover; however, recurrences are common. Often, bacterial infections in the bladder or urethra complicate matters. The veterinarian may prescribe medications and dietary changes to manage the condition (see page 44, Diet and Urinary Tract Health).

Recently, interstitial cystitis (IC), a chronic inflammatory disorder that mostly afflicts human females, has received closer scrutiny as a cause of urinary tract problems in cats, and ongoing research likely will benefit both species. In addition, many veterinarians believe that disruptive environmental factors, such as sudden or drastic changes in diet, weather, and household routine, may detrimentally influence urinary tract health as well.

Parasites

Internal parasites: The most common internal parasites that plague cats include roundworms, hookworms, and tapeworms. Heartworms, common in dogs, rarely infest cats, except in some humid regions, where the mosquito, the host organism, strongly prevails. In such high-risk areas, preventive prescription drugs may be warranted.

An infected queen can pass certain worms to her kittens through the placenta and through the breast milk. So, during your Somali's first visit to the veterinarian, request a stool analysis, which unveils the presence of most worms. Because deworming drugs can cause toxic reactions, they should be administered only under veterinary supervision. Prevention includes keeping cats indoors, maintaining good sanitation, and controlling fleas, lice, cockroaches, mosquitoes, and other vermin.

Kittens get roundworms from their infected mothers or through contact

reason, males are more prone to urinary tract blockages than females, although problems can occur in both sexes. In LUTD, often called FUS for feline urologic syndrome, tiny mineral crystals form in the lower urinary tract and irritate the internal tissues. In response to this discomfort, the cat may repeatedly lick its penis or vulva and dribble urine in unusual places, such as the bathtub. Feeling an uncomfortable urgency to urinate, it may visit the litter box frequently or miss the box altogether. The cat even may strain or cry as it attempts to void. Some people mistake this straining to urinate for constipation. If you notice these symptoms, or if you see blood in the urine, take your cat to a veterinarian immediately. If the crystals are large enough, they may block the urethra completely, creating a life-threatening emergency. If the cat cannot eliminate its urine, the kidneys may sustain irreversible damage with contaminated cat feces. Signs include vomiting, diarrhea, weight loss, a potbelly, and overall poor condition. Roundworms passed in vomit or stool look like white, wriggling spaghetti strands.

Hookworms are more prevalent in hot, humid areas. Cats pick up the larvae from infested soil, sometimes through their foot pads. Symptoms include anemia, diarrhea, weight loss, and black, tarry stools. Lungworms, acquired from contact with infected cats or from eating infected birds and rodents, migrate to a cat's lungs and cause a dry, persistent cough. Flukes, although uncommon, can be ingested by eating infected raw fish and other small prey. Cats allowed outdoors should be checked for worms during their annual physical checkups.

Tapeworms, the most common internal parasites found in adult cats, are transmitted by rodents and fleas. During grooming, cats ingest fleas, which carry the immature tapeworms in their intestines. The tapeworm larvae mature inside the cat's intestines, feeding on nutrients within. When passed in the stool, tapeworm segments look like white grains of rice. Some segments may stick to the hair around the anus, and when dry, they look like tiny seeds. Left untreated, tapeworms can rob the cat of important nutrients, but rarely cause any clinical signs. For effective treatment, combine deworming agents with appropriate flea control measures.

External parasites—fleas: Fleas are the most common external parasites to plague cats and frustrate their owners. Easy to spot, fleas leave behind evidence of their visits to the host in the form of "flea dirt," which looks like fine grains of black sand in the cat's fur. To inspect for flea dirt, rub your hand against your cat's fur along its back and near the neck and tail and look closely at the skin for tiny black

specks. Fleas feed on your cat's blood, and the pepper-like granules are flea excrement from digested blood. If dampened, the specks dissolve into bloody smudges. Left untreated, flea infestations can damage a cat's coat from excessive scratching and cause skin disorders, allergic reactions, and even anemia from blood loss.

Even indoor cats can get fleas from the yard that jump through window screens or ride in on a person's clothing or shoes. Once indoors, fleas lay eggs on the host. The eggs fall off your cat into carpets, upholstery, and bedding, where they hatch into larvae. The larvae grow and feed on debris among deep carpet fibers, an indoor environment that mimics their natural habitat— grass. Frequent vacuuming helps control this stage, but either throw out

Fleas can carry tapeworm larvae, which, when ingested by your Somali, grow into long, segmented strands inside the cat's intestines. Some segments break off and are eliminated in the cat's feces. The segments contain tapeworm embryos, which are consumed by flea larvae, beginning the life cycle anew.

HOW-TO:
Feline First Aid

Be Observant

Cats often conceal illness or pain, but observant owners can detect subtle behavior changes that cue them that all is not well. Early injury and disease detection can greatly improve treatment possibilities. Set aside time once a week to assess your cat's overall condition. Make a practice of inspecting your Somali for white teeth, pink gums, clean, pink ears, clear, bright eyes free of discharge, clean fur free of flea dirt, and a firm body free of lumps, bumps, and tender spots. By doing so regularly, you are more apt to notice anything out of the ordinary.

Be Prepared

Once recognized, the key to successfully coping with any emergency is to be prepared for it. Always keep your veterinarian's emergency number handy. In addition, assemble the following items in a first aid kit:
- a blanket or towel to wrap your cat in for warmth and safe restraint
- gauze pads and strips for bandaging
- peroxide (it's fresh if it bubbles) to clean wounds and induce vomiting
- syrup of ipecac to induce vomiting
- antibiotic ointment, such as Neosporin, for superficial wounds
- tweezers, handy for removing foreign objects from paw pads or from the throat, if the cat is choking
- ice pack for controlling swelling and bleeding
- scissors and adhesive tape
- artificial tears or sterile saline eye rinse to flush foreign material from eyes
- rectal thermometer, pediatric size

If an injured cat loses too much blood, it will suffer shock. Cover visible wounds with gauze or a clean towel and apply gentle, direct pressure to control bleeding.

Control Bleeding First

If an injured cat loses too much blood, it may go into shock and die before you reach a veterinary clinic. To control bleeding, cover visible wounds with gauze pads or some clean material and apply gentle, direct pressure over the site for several minutes. Do not attempt to splint or straighten fractured limbs.

How to Transport

It is important to remember the proper way to pick up an injured cat for transport to a veterinary hospital. *Never* pick up an injured animal by placing your hands under the belly. This will only make chest or abdominal injuries worse. If the cat is lying down, approach it from behind, slide one hand under the chest and one hand under the rump and gently place it in a pet carrier or on a blanket for transport. If the cat is crouched, grasp the scruff of the neck with one hand, place the other hand under the hips and rear legs for support, and cradle the cat in your arms. If the cat struggles, wrap it in a towel or blanket, leaving only the head sticking out. Remember, no matter how gentle your cat is, it may bite or

Be prepared for emergencies by keeping the following items handy in a first aid kit: blanket or towel, gauze pads, peroxide, syrup of ipecac, antibiotic ointment, tweezers, ice pack, scissors, adhesive tape, saline eye rinse, and an infant-size rectal thermometer.

claw you if it's in pain. Position an unconscious cat on its side for transport and keep it warm.

Accidental Poisoning

If you suspect your cat has ingested a potentially hazardous substance, read the package label to determine whether vomiting should be induced. If no label is available, do not induce vomiting unless an expert advises it—some substances can cause more harm when vomited back up. To induce vomiting, administer a small amount of syrup of ipecac by mouth with an eyedropper. Peroxide or salt water sometimes work, too. When possible, take the package and contents with you to the veterinarian.

For 24-hour assistance, seven days a week, call the National Animal Poison Control Information Center, operated by the University of Illinois. The hotline number is (800) 548-2423. The service charges a fee for each initial case, payable by credit card, but follow-ups are free. Those with short questions and those not wanting to use credit cards may have the charge added to their telephone bill by calling (900) 680-0000.

If your cat begins salivating heavily after you've applied a topical flea preparation to its fur, rinse the substance off immediately. Likewise, if your cat's coat becomes contaminated by bleach, pesticides, paint products, household cleaners, oil, tar, antifreeze, or other potential poisons, wash off immediately with pet shampoo or clip away the affected fur. If the coat is heavily saturated, seek veterinary help.

Never pick up an injured cat by placing your hands under the belly. This will make chest or abdominal injuries worse.

Foreign Objects

If the cat is salivating, gagging, and pawing at its mouth, it may be choking. First, open the mouth, attempt to pull out the tongue and look down the throat. If you can see the obstructing object, use tweezers to extract it. If the object does not readily dislodge, make no further attempt to remove it

without veterinary assistance. You may do more harm than good. Never poke tweezers into the eyes or ears; foreign objects here are best removed by a professional.

Heat Stroke, Frostbite

Heat stroke and frostbite require immediate medical attention. To prevent frostbite, keep your cat indoors and avoid overexposure during cold weather. To prevent heat stroke, never leave your cat in a parked car—not even for a few minutes, not even with the windows cracked. Temperatures inside a car climb too high for safe tolerance, even on mild days. With only hot air to breathe, your Somali can quickly suffer brain damage and die from heat stroke. Signs of heat stress include panting, vomiting, glazed eyes, rapid pulse, staggering, and red or purple tongue. Cool the body with tepid water, wrap in wet towels, and transport to a veterinary clinic immediately.

If the injured cat is lying down, approach from behind, slide one hand under the chest and one hand under the rump, and gently place the cat in a carrier or on a blanket for transport to the veterinarian.

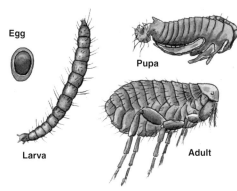

Egg

Pupa

Larva

Adult

Because fleas progress through four life stages—eggs, larvae, pupae, and adults—the most effective control measures include safe product combinations that kill adult fleas and prevent eggs and larvae from maturing.

the bag afterward, or suck up enough flea powder to coat the contents.

Pest control efforts fail if you concentrate only on killing adult fleas. Because the insects develop through four complex life stages—eggs, larvae, pupae, adults—your arsenal must include sprays, powders, or foggers targeted to kill fleas at various life cycles. Flea foggers, for example, treat entire rooms with a penetrating blast of insecticide, but if you select one that kills only adults, you miss the immature stages ready to hatch soon in your carpets. Shop for foggers that contain an insect growth regulator (IGR), a chemical that stops the eggs and larvae from fully developing and offers some residual effect. Because most compounds do not penetrate the hard-shell pupal stage, repeat all indoor treatments in two weeks to kill the emerging adults. Severe infestations may require a professional exterminator's services. Used as directed, IGRs are considered safe, and many on-pet products now contain these compounds for better flea control.

Before activating flea foggers, remove cats and other animals from the envi-

ronment. Cover or remove foodstuffs, as well as food and water dishes, so they will not be contaminated by the spray. Thoroughly air out the room(s), according to the label directions, before allowing animals to reenter.

If you are not comfortable with the idea of using pesticides in your home or on your pet, sodium borate compounds offer a less toxic alternative for carpeted areas. Marketed through pet retail and mail-order firms, borates—white, powdered salts of boric acid—apparently hamper flea reproduction by contaminating their food supply. The substance acts as a stomach poison on flea larvae feeding on treated carpets, halting further life-cycle development. However, borates have only limited effect on adult fleas through desiccation. For this reason, the "clearing out" process is slow, taking from two to five weeks to eliminate an infestation while adult fleas die off naturally. Being water-soluble, borates are useless for outdoor flea control, and likewise, dissolve to ineffectiveness when you shampoo the carpets.

In addition to treating carpets and upholstered furniture, flea control involves bathing the cat, washing or replacing pet bedding and spraying the lawn. An endless array of sprays, dips, powders, shampoos, and flea collars clutters the market. So, when choosing one chemical to use on your Somali and another to treat its environment, be careful to select products that can be combined safely. To avoid potentially toxic combinations, ask your veterinarian to recommend appropriate flea control products.

Also ask about a new once-a-month oral medication, PROGRAM (lufenuron), recently approved for use in cats. The drug, available by prescription through veterinarians, causes female fleas living on the host to produce infertile eggs. Male fleas are unaffected, and fleas must bite the host for the drug to work. For these reasons, the drug is useful in controlling indoor infestations, but it is not a cure-all for cats that suffer allergic reactions to flea bites.

Use only products labeled specifically for cats and follow the directions carefully. Select flea collars that have elastic or breakaway sections to prevent strangling, in case the cat gets caught on an object. Let flea collars air out a few days before putting them on your cat. Do not use any product on a kitten or debilitated cat without veterinary approval.

If you do not like the idea of spraying pesticides on your yard, consider the environmentally friendly flea-eating nematodes available at feed stores and pet shops. When sprayed on your lawn, these microscopic "bugs" destroy flea larvae without harming beneficial insects, children, or animals. One application lasts about a month.

Other external parasites: Besides fleas, cats sometimes play host to ticks, lice, and mites. Ticks burrow their heads into the skin and suck blood. Remove them promptly by grasping the body as close to the skin as possible with tweezers, then pulling straight out (without twisting) with firm, gentle traction. Because some ticks carry Lyme disease, which humans can catch, care should be taken to control them if your cat goes outdoors. Ask your veterinarian to recommend a suitable insecticide. Some flea collars help control ticks.

Uncommon in well-kept, healthy cats, lice look like white specks (nits) stuck to the fur or buried beneath mats on poorly groomed animals. Clipping the coat and bathing with a medicated shampoo gets rid of them. Mites, being microscopic, are harder to see, but signs of their presence include itchiness, hair loss, crusty sores, scaly dandruff, and body odor. A veterinarian needs to identify the specific mite variety before prescribing treatment.

Periodically swab the outer part of your Somali's ears to keep them clean and pink, but never poke the cotton tip into the ear canal.

Ear mites: The most common mite found on cats is the ear mite, which lives in the ear canal and produces a crumbly, dark brown, foul-smelling, waxy discharge. Healthy ears should be clean and pink inside; therefore, if you notice waxy buildup and see your Somali shaking its head and scratching its ears, suspect ear mites. Prompt veterinary attention prevents spread to the inner ear, where an infection can cause loss of balance and ultimately deafness. Because ear mites are contagious, other cats and dogs in the household may require treatment as well.

Skin Problems

Ringworm is not caused by a worm at all, but rather by a fungus. Signs include scaly skin and patchy hair loss. Because people can catch this skin infection from cats, prompt veterinary treatment and disinfection of pet bedding are essential. Treatment may include clipping the coat, bathing the skin, and administering topical or oral medications. A new vaccine is available, so discuss this option with your veterinarian.

Flea allergy dermatitis: Some cats are so allergic to flea saliva that the bite from a single flea will send them into a frenzy, scratching, biting, and licking to get at the culprit. The severe itching lasts long after the flea leaves, so you may never even see a parasite on the pet. Such sensitivity can lead to an uncomfortable skin condition called flea allergy dermatitis. Besides itchiness, other symptoms include hair loss, patchy redness (called "hot spots"), and scabby, crusty sores on the skin. In addition to prescribed medications, aggressive and diligent flea control measures lessen the condition's severity and occurrence.

Other Allergies

Like people, cats can be allergic to a host of things in their environment, including pollen, weeds, grasses, mold spores, house dust, feathers, wool,

Because Somalis are prone to gingivitis (gum inflamation), regular toothbrushing and good dental care are a must.

insect stings, drugs, chemicals, and food ingredients. But instead of sneezing, watery eyes, and runny noses, cats' symptoms more likely involve itchy skin, face, and ears. Typical warning signs include rubbing against furniture or carpet and excessive scratching, licking, or chewing at itchy places. Gastrointestinal symptoms like vomiting and diarrhea also can occur, particularly if the allergen, or allergy-causing substance, is ingested in a food or drug. Redness, crusty skin, and hair loss around the nose, mouth, and face suggests a food allergy, or even an allergy to plastic feeding dishes. In the latter case, replacing plastic dishes with ceramic or stainless steel ones offers an easy remedy.

Unfortunately, most allergy cases are not so simple. Testing exists, but allergies remain difficult to diagnose. Treatment varies widely from patient to patient, depending on the cause and symptoms, and may include antihistamines or other medications, supplemental fatty acids, or even allergy shots. Recovery can take a long time, and because allergies usually persist for a lifetime, owners must commit to avoiding or reducing the allergen in the cat's environment for as long as it lives.

Tooth and Gum Care

Somalis, like their Abyssinian sisters, seem prone to gingivitis, or inflamed gums. Healthy gums are pink; diseased gums are tender, red, and swollen. Neglected dental disease allows bacteria to leak into the bloodstream from sore, infected gums, compromising your cat's immune system and overall health. Plaque and tartar buildup on the teeth cause gingivitis. Left untreated, the gums begin to recede gradually and the teeth loosen. Besides bad breath, a cat with dental problems may have difficulty eating because its teeth and gums hurt. As a result, it may lose weight and condition. A cat with sensitive teeth also may flinch when you try to stroke the side of its face. The best way to prevent such discomfort is to regularly brush or rinse your cat's teeth with oral hygiene products designed for veterinary use. From time to time, it may be necessary to have your cat's teeth professionally cleaned. For this procedure, the cat is anesthetized, and the veterinarian uses an ultrasonic scaler to blast away the ugly, brown tartar and polish the teeth.

Toothbrushing

To get your Somali accustomed to having its mouth gently opened and handled, start early, while it's still a kitten. An older cat takes more time to train and may never be completely cooperative. Ask your veterinarian to demonstrate proper brushing technique. Then, for the first week or so, dip your finger in something tasty, such as canned cat food juice, and gently rub the cat's teeth and gums.

Purchase a small pet toothbrush with ultra-soft bristles or one designed to fit over your finger tip for easier use. Also, select a non-foaming, enzymatic toothpaste made especially for animals. These pastes, designed to dissolve plaque without a lot of scrubbing action, come in fish, poultry, and malt flavors for finicky felines. *Never* use human toothpaste on a cat because it burns the back of the throat.

Try brushing only a few teeth on one side at first. If your cat doesn't accept the brush right away, wrap gauze around your finger and gently massage the teeth and gums. With each try, brush a few more teeth, until your cat accepts the process without a fuss. If the cat struggles, don't force it to submit. Instead, be extra gentle and patient, so it won't learn to dread having its mouth handled. Offer lots of praise when the cat willingly lets you brush, even if only briefly.

Medicating Your Somali

Getting your Somali used to having its mouth opened and handled will make it much easier for you to give it pills, should the need arise. Otherwise, the ordeal is likely to be a two-person job. If necessary, restrain the cat by wrapping its body in a towel with only the head sticking out. To medicate your cat, grasp the head with your thumb and index finger on its cheekbones and tilt back the head. Pry open the jaws with your finger, drop the pill into the back of the throat, then hold the cat's mouth shut and stroke its throat until it swallows.

To administer liquid medication, tilt the head back, insert an eyedropper into the corner of the mouth and gently

To medicate your Somali, grasp the head with your thumb and index finger on its cheekbones and tilt back the head. Gently pry open the jaws and drop the pill into the back of the throat.

Hold the cat's mouth shut and stroke its throat until it swallows.

A paper bag makes a safe and suitable toy or hideout for a cat, but because of the danger of suffocation, never offer plastic bags.

squirt in a few drops at a time. Do not squirt the medication into the cat's mouth too quickly or too forcefully, as the cat may inhale the liquid. Hold the mouth shut until the cat swallows. Some medications can be mixed in the cat's food, if they are not too bitter tasting. Make sure other animals do not consume the food.

If your cat's condition calls for injections, eye ointments, ear drops, or force-feeding that you must do at home, your veterinarian will explain and demonstrate the best method. Make sure you understand how and when to administer any medication before you attempt to do it yourself, and know what to expect in terms of recovery time and side effects.

Never give your Somali any over-the-counter painkillers for humans, such as aspirin and especially acetaminophen, which can be deadly to cats.

Hair Ball Prevention
Because cats lick their fur to clean themselves, the swallowed hair accumulates in the stomach. Normally, this creates no problem as the hair mass moves through the digestive tract and gets eliminated in the usual way. However, if the mass becomes too dense, it may cause a blockage, requiring an enema or even surgery to remove it. Signs of a blockage include frequent vomiting and refusal to eat.

Frequently, cats spit up tubular masses of ingested hair, called hair balls. Before the cat vomits a hair ball, it will crouch and cough a few times in a dry, hacking, wheezing manner. Except for the mess, vomiting a hair ball is no cause for concern, unless it becomes too frequent, in which case you need to offer some remedy.

To prevent hair balls, groom your Somali regularly. Brushing and combing removes the dead hair it would swallow otherwise. But if your cat displays the typical "hair ball cough," administer one of various petroleum-based hair ball remedies recommended by your veterinarian. Or dab some plain petroleum jelly on your cat's paw to lick off. These products help lubricate the hair mass so that it expels more easily. Grass also seems to act as a purgative to help cats expel excess hair from the stomach. You can grow a fresh supply of grass indoors for your cat, and some pet stores sell grass kits for this purpose. Providing some greenery for your cat to nibble on also may help keep it away from your house plants.

Vital Signs
Taking a cat's temperature is a procedure most of them do not take to kindly and it is best left to your veterinarian. However, at times, it may be necessary for you to do it yourself. To take a cat's temperature, use a rectal thermometer designed for human infants. Shake the mercury down to well below 100°F (38°C). Lubricate the thermometer with petroleum jelly and, while restraining the cat, insert with a gentle twisting motion into the anus about an inch. Hold in place for two

minutes. Wipe clean to read. Normal temperature is 100 to 102.5°F (37.8–39°C). Any higher is cause for concern. To take a cat's pulse, feel for it high up on the inside hind leg. Normal pulse rate ranges from 100 to 180 beats per minute. Normal respiration is 20 to 30 breaths per minute.

Euthanasia and Pet Loss

The sad part of pet ownership is that cats do not live as long as humans do. Eventually, we have to say good-bye. Although difficult and painful, the decision to euthanize a cat is sometimes the last and kindest gift we can offer a long-time friend suffering or debilitated from illness, injury, or old age. An anesthetic overdose administered by a veterinarian simply "puts the cat to sleep" without pain. Some veterinarians allow owners who request it to remain with the cat during the brief procedure, and many help handle cremation or burial arrangements.

For many people, losing a cherished cat companion causes as much trauma and heartbreak as losing a human loved one. The grieving process is essentially the same, but some people simply don't understand how much it hurts to lose a pet. These folks may make well-meaning but misguided comments, such as, "It was only a cat! Just get another one!" that belittle the special bond you had with your cat. Don't listen to them. Instead, talk to people who understand your grief. Some cities even have pet grief counseling and support groups to help people through this crisis. Ask your veterinarian for details.

Giving another cat a good home is a beautiful way to honor your deceased friend's memory; however, allow time to grieve over your loss first. Another cat will not replace the one you lost, but when you feel ready, another cat can build a new relationship with you that will be as uniquely special and joyful as the previous one.

Understanding Somali Cats

The Somali Personality

Affectionate and extroverted, Somalis crave and thrive on human companionship. They tend to follow their special person from room to room, investigating all the goings-on. And like any other family member, they enjoy spending most of their time in the rooms where you spend yours. When reared in a loving environment, Somalis do not fear strangers. They cheerfully greet and rub against guests as if saying, "Any friend of yours is a friend of mine." Active and athletic, Somalis love to climb and jump. High places, such as refrigerator tops and bookcases, are favorite lounging sites. So secure your valuable vases and other breakable knickknacks. Many Somalis like to play in water and will entertain themselves for hours if you leave a faucet barely trickling for them. Some have even been known to hop in the bathtub with their owners! Alert and intelligent, Somalis learn tricks quickly and display excellent memory and problem-solving skills. After watching how you open doors and drawers, they will put their busy paws to the task and soon figure out how to gain entrance on their own. For these reasons, Somali households must be made "child-proof."

Reading body language: Happy and friendly (top left), timid or submissive (top right), frightened or defensive (bottom right), angry and aggressive (bottom left).

Somali Body Language

Somalis can communicate eloquently with their feline and human companions. As the owner, you need to know how to interpret your cat's body language so you can judge its moods. When your Somali is happy to see you, it approaches with ears pricked forward and tail held high. At the sight of a stranger, a timid or submissive cat crouches, lowers its ears, and drops its tail. A frightened or defensive cat makes itself appear as big as possible by arching its back and bristling its fur to full fluff. An angry cat crouches low, as if poised to attack. It flicks its tail from side to side, flattens its ears, and sometimes hisses loudly or utters a low, drawn-out growl as a warning.

Often, cats that know each other well will play and move through these stances in a seemingly ferocious manner. Their playful encounters usually culminate in a gleeful chase through the house. These mock fights help them stay fit and keep their skills honed for the real thing. In an actual confrontation, two cats may remain tense and still for several minutes, usually until one makes a strategic withdrawal. Being sensible creatures, cats generally observe territorial good manners and avoid unnecessary fighting.

Vocal Language

Although cats have an extensive vocal repertoire, Somalis rarely speak aloud, unless they have an urgent need to communicate something to their caretakers, such as "It's way past my dinner time, and I'm starving!" They will lead you to their empty food bowl, then look up at you and mew pitifully. Generally, the more urgent the request, the louder the meow. A loud, throaty howl can mean your cat feels distressed—maybe it's gotten accidentally shut in a closet. Females in heat belt out a particularly annoying yowl, and mother cats chirp softly when calling their kittens. According to the intonation, a cat's meow can express many moods and needs. In time, your Somali will train you to understand its personal vocabulary of sounds and body postures. Soon, you will find yourself talking back and swearing that your Somali understands every word you say. Learning this species-to-species communication is fun because it's almost like sharing a secret language. It's also an important part of the bonding process between cats and humans, and ideally, you will come to

feel that no one else can understand or care for your cat as well as you do.

Purring

The most beloved feline sound is the purr, thought to be produced by vibrations in the vocal cords as the cat breathes in and out. One of many simple pleasures of cat ownership, relaxing with a purring cat in your lap relieves stress, promotes a mutual sense of comfort, and strengthens the human/feline bond. However, it's a common misconception that purring always indicates pleasure or contentment. While it's true that cats purr when they feel happy, secure, warm, and well-fed, they also purr when hungry, upset, sick, or in pain, possibly to calm and comfort themselves. Cats have even been known to purr while dying.

Your Somali's Senses

Much of the mystery associated with cats results from the unique anatomy of their five senses, which are far superior to ours. Understanding how your Somali perceives its world helps explain many behaviors that seem incomprehensible otherwise.

Sight: Cats possess poor color vision, but they see well in dim light. Uniquely suited to hunting and stalking, their eyes are especially adept at detecting slight movements made by prey animals. A stalking cat will crouch patiently for long periods, staring at seemingly nothing, until its camouflaged prey finally reveals its whereabouts with barely a twitch. A special layer of cells behind the retina, called the *tapetum lucidum*, makes a cat's eyes appear to glow in the dark. These cells act like a mirror, reflecting all available light back onto the retina and giving the cat its exceptional night vision.

Furthermore, the feline pupil can dilate much wider than the human eye, allowing the cat's eye to collect light

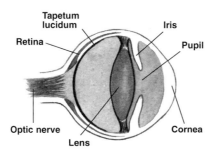

The tapetum lucidum, *a special cell layer behind the retina, magnifies light in dim conditions and makes a cat's eyes glow in the dark.*

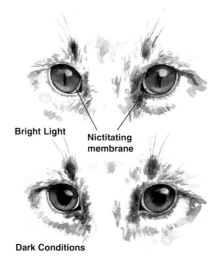

more effectively in dim conditions. To help it detect threatening movements over a wider area, a frightened or defensive cat dilates its pupils. On sunny days, a cat's pupils constrict to vertical slits to block out bright light.

Another special characteristic of the cat's eye is an opaque third eyelid, called the nictitating membrane, which helps protect and lubricate the eyeball. Although usually not visible under normal conditions, except occasionally when the cat is sleeping, the third eyelid protrudes from the eye's inside corner if the eye gets injured, irritated, or infected. The appearance of this film over the eyes also occurs with some diseases and warrants a veterinary examination if it persists beyond an occasional blink.

Smell: Cats possess an acute sense of smell. When two cats meet, they sniff each other about the head and anal area, where scent glands exude a myriad of personal information. Often, a cat greets a human friend in similar fashion, jumping in a person's lap to sniff the face, then turning to present its rear end for examination. Like many other mammals, cats have a special scent mechanism, called the vomeronasal or Jacobson's organ, in the roof of their mouths behind the incisor teeth that allows them to "taste" odor molecules. When using this organ, a cat curls its upper lip back and sniffs the air deeply with teeth bared and mouth partially agape. This odd-looking grimace is called the "flehmen response." Cats often display flehmen when examining urine and scent marks left by other animals. Researchers believe the special organ helps mammals find mates by sorting out sex-related scent hormones called pheromones.

Taste: Well-known for their finicky eating habits, cats have a discriminating sense of taste. Once developed, their taste preferences can be difficult to change. A cat fed the same food all its life may steadfastly refuse any sort of dietary change, even if its health depends on it. To avoid creating this finicky behavior, alternate a few varieties of cat foods and flavors from kittenhood on.

Cats can easily detect medications added to their food and usually eat around the edges or refuse the food altogether. For this reason, ask your veterinarian to show you how to put pills or liquids directly in your Somali's mouth (see also Medicating Your Somali, page 63).

Touch: It's been said that if a cat's whiskers can pass through a small opening, the cat knows its body will fit through, too. While this may be more fancy than fact, particularly in the case of fat cats whose bellies are broader than their whisker breadth, it is true that whiskers are highly sensitive tactile organs. Cats use them to gauge the size of prey caught in their paws, to avoid objects in dim light, and to detect vibrations and changes in their environment. For these reasons, never clip your Somali's whiskers.

Hearing: Because its normal prey typically emits high-pitched sounds, a cat's ears are tuned to frequencies well beyond the range of human hearing. When a cat hears something, it swivels its ears toward the source and looks in the direction of the noise. Cats learn to respond to certain words by recognizing the sounds of the first few letters, and your Somali will quickly learn its name if you consistently call to it in the same tone of voice at feeding time.

Balance and the Righting Reflex

If a cat rolls off a windowsill and falls in an upside-down position, a balance mechanism in the inner ear enables it to rotate the forehand first, then the hindquarters, so that it rights itself in mid-air and lands on all fours. However, this remarkable reflex ability does not mean that cats can fall from great heights without injury. On the contrary, enough sustain fractures in falls from poorly-screened apartment windows during hot weather to give such incidents a name already mentioned on page 32—high-rise syndrome.

Hunting Habits

As natural predators, cats are well-adapted with excellent vision for night hunting in near darkness. Typically, they catnap throughout the day and awake ready for action by evening. By bedtime, their hunting instincts rev into high gear, and your toes wriggling under the bed covers present the perfect prey to pounce upon. This nocturnal tendency probably contributed to the time-honored tradition of "putting

The righting reflex: an inner ear balance mechanism enables the cat to rotate its forehand first, then the hindquarters, so that it usually, but not always, lands on all fours from a fall.

69

HOW-TO:
Treating Elimination Problems

Causes

Contrary to what some people believe, cats do not eliminate outside of the litter box out of spite. Generally, when a housebroken cat eliminates outside its litter box, it is either marking territory or displaying a preference for a particular spot, surface or litter material. Often, the behavior is symptomatic of anxiety or physical discomfort. Whenever a cat begins eliminating in inappropriate places, consider urinary tract infections and other medical causes first. Prompt veterinary treatment can reverse the problem before it becomes an established habit. Once disease is ruled out, pursue the behavioral approaches.

Solutions

Because the motivating factors usually are different, it's important to determine whether the cat is spraying vertical surfaces or squatting to urinate on horizontal surfaces. Sometimes the sight of outdoor cats or the introduction of a new pet or a new baby into the household can trigger territorial spraying. Often, veterinarians can prescribe drugs that ease anxiety and help suppress spraying and aggressive behaviors. However, a cat that squats on the carpet or floor may simply be expressing a dislike for the location of its litter box or for the texture of the litter. Perhaps the box is near a noisy furnace that frightens the cat when it is operating.

Try moving the box to a quieter area, or if possible, place it at or near the site of the "accident." For whatever reason, the cat may prefer that spot, and putting the box there may solve the problem. If location doesn't seem to be a factor, experiment with different litter materials; some cats don't like litters treated with perfumes and deodorizers. Often, a problem arises because cat and owner have different opinions as to what constitutes a clean litter box. After all, digging in dirty, damp litter is like using an unflushed toilet. Be fastidious about removing urine and feces daily and replacing soiled litter weekly, and your cat will be more happily inclined to continue using the box.

The number of cats in a household can influence spraying and elimination behaviors. If you have more than one cat, provide each with its own litter box. Sometimes the more aggressive cat will chase another away from the litter box. If this happens, place the boxes far enough apart, even in separate rooms, to give each cat a sense of privacy and individual territory.

Whatever the cause, punishing a cat for spraying or eliminating in inappropriate places is seldom effective and often makes matters worse. Rubbing your cat's nose in the mess will only make it fear you. Spanking it, then carrying it to the litter box may backfire and actually cause it to develop a fear of the litter box.

How to Clean Up

To deter the cat from using the same location as a toilet again, clean up accidents with enzymatic products that dissolve the odor. Remember to clean the mat under the carpet, too, as the urine will have

A Somali that stands on the sides of the litter box, steps gingerly in and out, or rarely digs in the litter may be expressing a dislike for the type of litter in use. Try different brands and textures.

Disturbing noises or foot traffic near the litter box may make the cat develop a dislike for that location. Move the box to a quieter, more private, area.

screen, or double-sided sticky tape. If possible, keep the cat completely away from the area for awhile to break the habit. For further reinforcement, use a water pistol or make a loud noise to startle the cat away from the area every time you see it near the spot. For a different approach, try changing the significance of the area by placing food and water bowls there. Cats typically will not eliminate where they eat.

Cats are fastidiously clean creatures. If you're equally fastidious about removing urine and feces from the box daily, your Somali likely will reward you with good litter box behavior.

soaked through. Any traces of scent left will attract the cat back to the same spot. If you can't lift the carpet to clean under it, use a syringe to inject solution under the rug. Several good odor neutralizing products can be purchased at pet shops. Vinegar and water works fairly well, too. But avoid ammonia-based cleaners. Ammonia is a urine byproduct and might attract the cat back to the spot.

After you thoroughly clean the spot, make the surface less appealing to the cat by covering it temporarily with plastic, aluminum foil, sandpaper, window

Fawn kitten. Cats have excellent hearing, and Somalis in particular are noted for their large, impressive ears. (Photo courtesy of American Greetings Corporation, © AGC, Inc.)

the cat out" at night, no doubt so that a weary owner could get some sleep. Fortunately, indoor cats adapt readily to our diurnal timetables, and many sleep soundly all night on their owners' beds, doubling as fail-safe alarm clocks come morning. As with people, cats that get plenty of exercise sleep better.

To discourage disturbing nocturnal ramblings, play with your Somali in the evening, a few hours before bedtime. Help it burn off excess energy with interactive toys, like a kitty fishing pole with sparklers or feathers attached. Throw out the line and slowly reel in your Somali as it stalks the lure. Observe your Somali honing its hunting skills as it crouches and creeps forward silently, pupils wide and eyes fixed, watching for the slightest move that might mean the "prey" is going to run. Muscles remain tensed and ready for instant pursuit. The tail twitches in anticipation. As the cat prepares to

pounce, it wriggles its rear, treading quietly with the back legs, as if testing which foot will provide the better spring action. Before the feather flutters one last time, the cat springs upon it with claws extended, the front paws striking in deadly accuracy to pinion the prey. One well-placed bite with the powerful canine teeth ends the struggle.

Even people who despise predation confess to being entertained and awed by the cat's fluid body coordination and rigid concentration during play sessions. The ancient Egyptians worshipped the cat for its unequaled rodent control talents, yet modern-day cat enthusiasts often experience a paradoxical twinge of guilt when their pet's natural instincts bring down a fledgling sparrow. Worse for some people are the times when their outdoor cat brings home prey as a gift offering and deposits the dead body on the doorstep. Experts say this normal behavior relates to the way cats per-

Although cats have an extensive repertoire of vocal sounds, they communicate mostly through body language.

ceive their human caretakers as family members. Mother cats instinctively bring dead or stunned prey to the nest when they teach their kittens how to recognize and hunt prey. So if your Somali delivers a similar offering to your "nest," don't punish it for behaving naturally. Simply praise the cat for its generosity, then dispose of the "gift" quickly so that your Somali will have no further exposure to parasites or disease carried by the prey. If predation disgusts you, you can prevent it by keeping your cat indoors. Your Somali certainly will remain healthier without exposure to diseased rodents or birds and other outdoor hazards, and it

will be just as happy hunting and preying on store-bought catnip mice.

Territorial Marking

Rubbing: Cats greet their owners by rubbing against their legs, but this endearing habit is more than an expression of affection. It is one means of territorial marking. By rubbing against furniture and other objects, cats leave behind scent from glands around their faces, mouths, and tails. Humans can't smell the scent, but other cats can. Because you're part of your cat's territory, your Somali really is saying, "You belong to

When your Somali rubs against you affectionately, it is really marking you with its scent and claiming you as part of its territory.

me!" when it rubs against you and marks you with its scent. In addition, the mingling of your smell on the cat's fur helps identify you as part of its circle of friends.

Spraying: Less endearing is the feline habit of spraying urine to mark territory. Although males are more prone to this behavior, females some-

Spraying differs from simple elimination in that the cat backs up to a vertical surface, raises the tail, and, while standing, squirts urine to mark territory. In simple elimination, a cat squats to urinate on a horizontal surface.

times do it to communicate their reproductive status, especially when in heat. Although spaying and neutering tend to curb this undesirable behavior, both sexes, whether whole or altered, may occasionally resort to spraying when engaged in a dispute with another cat over territory or dominance.

When a cat sprays, it stands, rather than squats, with its back to a vertical surface and with its tail straight in the air. The tail quivers as the cat squirts urine to mark the wall, drapery or furniture leg.

Clawing: When a cat scratches the arm of the couch, it is not misbehaving. It is fulfilling an instinctive need to keep its basic defense weaponry—its claws—sharp and trim. Similar to filing fingernails, the in-and-out action on wood or rough fabric helps strip away the dead, outer layers of the claws. The action also marks the scratched object with scent from glands in the cat's paws. The scent, plus an apparent preference for the spot, draws the cat back to the same site to claw until the couch arm becomes a shredded mess. You cannot eliminate this natural behavior, but you can modify it by teaching the cat to use a scratching post as an alternative to clawing your furniture (see Scratching Posts, page 29). To avoid destructive clawing habits, begin training your kitten to use a scratching post as soon as you bring it home.

Another alternative for dealing with clawing problems is to glue vinyl nail caps onto the cat's newly trimmed claws. The caps give the nails a soft, blunt tip and help prevent the destruction of carpets, furniture, and draperies. The major drawback to this method is that the vinyl caps have to be reapplied every four to six weeks, as the nails grow out. The application is simple, however, and owners can purchase take-home kits and learn to manicure their cats' nails themselves. Ask your veterinarian to demonstrate the product. Vinyl nail caps are not recommended for outdoor animals because they inhibit a cat's ability to climb.

Declawing

Declawing is the least desirable alternative for dealing with destructive clawing and should be considered only as a last resort after other methods have failed. Banned in some countries, this controversial procedure involves putting the cat under anesthesia and surgically amputating the claw tip and the last bone of the toe. Generally, only the front claws are removed, because the hind feet are not used for scratching furniture. After the operation, the cat suffers some pain as its mutilated paws heal.

Declawing renders a cat ineligible for some show rings, because many cat associations that sponsor shows oppose the practice. With only the front claws removed, a cat still can use its rear claws to climb trees. Yet, declawing inhibits a cat's ability to climb and defend itself against attackers to a degree. Cats allowed to roam outdoors have a clear disadvantage and, therefore, should not be declawed. Many people believe that robbing a cat of its natural defenses in this way harms it psychologically and may make it more apt to bite. Some owners report profound personality changes in their cats after the surgery, including inappropriate toilet habits, brought on perhaps by litter irritating the tender incisions. Older cats seem to have more difficulty adjusting to life without claws than kittens.

Multicat Households

Owning more than one cat brings its own special joys. You get to compare and savor each feline's unique personality as they vie for your attention. In addition, two cats can keep each other company while the owner is at work all day. Despite their aloof, solitary reputa-

Declawing involves surgical amputation of the claw tips and the last bone of the toes.

tion, cats clearly enjoy companionship and are highly social. They generally adapt well to group living; however, confining too many cats in a limited space increases the incidence of behavior problems. Signs of stress from overcrowding may include hiding, fighting, house-soiling, and excessive grooming.

Often, what people perceive as a behavior "problem" in the home is quite normal for cats in the wild. For instance, cats, being naturally territorial, mark and defend areas where they spend most of their time. Fortunately, when living in social groups, cats tend to claim less territory, and boundaries become more flexible. Individuals that bond as friends share space, sleep together and groom each other. In general, the bigger your home, the fewer territorial problems your cats are likely to develop indoors. But if you have only so much room, expand the cats' available territory from floor to ceiling by installing vertical cat-climbing trees and carpeted kitty condos. In addition, carpet-covered cat trees with tiered sleeping shelves make excellent scratching posts and satisfy the Somali's urge to roost in high places.

Grooming Your Somali

Although Somalis have long, silky fur, they do not require the daily grooming commitment that some other longhaired breeds, such as the Persian and the Himalayan, demand. This lucky long-hair-without-the-fuss feature is part of the Somali's "best of both worlds" charm touted by breeders and fanciers alike. Nevertheless, even if you never intend to show your Somali, it still needs regular grooming and occasional bathing to keep the coat clean and mat-free. Furthermore, regular grooming is the best and least expensive way to prevent hair-ball problems in longhaired cats. Brushing also helps stimulate circulation and distribute natural oils through the coat, keeping it shiny and healthy looking.

A cat's coat consists of a topcoat of long "guard" hairs over a soft under-coat of "down" and "awn" hairs. The coarser guard hairs protect the dense underfur from the elements. The soft down hairs closest to the skin provide added warmth, while the awn hairs form a middle layer of insulation. The guard and awn hairs also can fluff out to trap air for better insulation. The Somali's coat is usually two to three inches (5–7 cm) long, and the texture varies in individuals from dense and woolly to long and silky.

Shedding

In addition to keeping the coat clean and mat-free, regular grooming mini-mizes the amount of cat hair left on your furniture and clothing. While shed-ding is most noticeable in spring and fall, during the seasonal changes of hair coat, house cats living in artificial light shed a little bit year-round. Many people believe seasonal temperature changes cause cats to shed, but experts say environmental lighting gov-erns the process. Under natural condi-tions, the lengthening sunlight hours in early spring trigger the cat's body to shed hair and grow a new coat in preparation for the changing season. Similarly, autumn's shorter daylight hours cause the coat to thicken for win-ter. But when artificial lighting extends the daylight hours in the cat's environ-ment year-round, this natural cycle seems to get confused. The result is a

When combing the throat and chest, raise the chin a little and stroke upward.

coat that sheds slightly on a continual basis. In addition, overheated homes in winter may make some house cats prone to shed more than normal because their skin gets too dry.

If your Somali's skin ever appears too dry or flaky, or if the coat appears dull, looks oily, smells bad, or feels brittle, schedule a visit to your veterinarian. A number of medical and dietary problems can affect the skin and hair coat, including allergies, parasites, and hormonal imbalances, among others. Proper nutrition is especially important, because the Somali's soft coat tends to dry out if the diet lacks essential fats. Also, as cats enter their late teens, they require more grooming assistance, because their decreasing flexibility makes them less able to do a good self-grooming job.

First Steps in Grooming

Most cats love the attention they get during grooming and learn to tolerate their beauty sessions readily if you accustom them to the procedure early and if you make each experience pleasurable. Starting while your Somali is still a kitten, spend a few minutes each day gently combing the fur with a small, fine-toothed comb. Keep the sessions short until your kitten gets used to being handled this way. Use the opportunity to get your Somali accustomed to having its mouth gently opened, its ears handled, and its paws touched. This extra effort will pay off later when brushing teeth, administering medications, cleaning ears, and trimming claws (see pages 62–63 for dental care tips). Don't attempt to restrain your Somali if its attention wanders elsewhere. Simply end the session and try again later. Practice this daily for several weeks, then after your kitten accepts grooming graciously, you can cut back the number of sessions gradually to once or twice a week.

Use a wide-toothed comb on the tail, gently working from base to tip.

Clipping your cat's claws helps minimize snags in furnishings and clothing.

While grooming, hold the kitten in your lap, or place it on a counter or table. Establish a regular grooming location and routine, and your Somali will quickly learn what's expected of it when you take it to that spot and pick up the comb. As your kitten grows, graduate to a medium-size comb, and by adulthood, switch to a larger, wide-toothed steel comb. For convenience and versatility, some combs come with closely-spaced teeth on one end and widely-spaced teeth on the other end. Use the fine-toothed end on the shorter hair around the face, head, and chin. Use it also as a flea comb, handily trapping the parasites and their dirt in the closely-spaced teeth. To dispatch the fleas, simply dip the comb in a nearby pan of water until the insects drown.

Always end grooming sessions with a brief playtime, lots of praise, and maybe even a special treat, and your cat will eagerly anticipate the next one.

Combing and Brushing Methods

When combing, start at the base of the neck and gently comb the back and sides. Raise the chin a little to comb the throat and chest. When combing delicate areas, such as the belly, legs, and tail, be especially careful not to rake the comb's teeth against the cat's sensitive skin. To strip the coat during shedding season, comb long fur upward, against the way the hair lies. Called *back-combing*, this method removes the dead undercoat trapped closer to the skin and helps prevent matting. To put the hair back in place, comb through it a second time, going the way the hair lies.

If you plan to show your Somali, you want to keep it in full coat and avoid stripping out too much undercoat. Stripping out too much undercoat can make the entire coat look flat instead of full. So, to avoid thinning a show coat, comb *with* the lie of the

fur. Also, because hair left in the comb pulls even more hair, remove the fur caught in the teeth after each swipe. Because brush bristles can break the delicate hairs, some breeders recommend using them sparingly. To reduce breakage and static, choose a soft, natural bristle brush for the task.

To add volume and fullness to the tail, gently back-comb, starting at the tail base close to the body and working toward the tip. Gently fluff the tail, lifting the hair and combing upward toward the body. To avoid stripping the fragile tail hairs, use only a wide-toothed comb and remove hair from the comb as you work.

If the coat appears oily in spots, sprinkle some talcum or baby powder on the fur, work it in, then brush it out thoroughly. The powder absorbs the oil, separates the clumped hairs, and leaves the fur feeling soft and clean. Pet stores also sell dry shampoos for this purpose.

Intact males are particularly prone to develop an oily condition called "stud tail," caused by overactive glands and characterized by a waxy brown buildup at the base and top ridge of the tail. If not periodically cleansed, the greasy accumulation can form a crust on the skin and infect the hair follicles, causing sores and hair loss on the tail. Neutering generally relieves the condition.

Removing Mats

Fortunately, the Somali coat is of a length and texture that renders it relatively mat-free. Except for an occasional mat in the "armpits" or on the belly, this particular grooming problem, more prevalent in some other long-haired breeds, seldom afflicts the Somali. It's important to understand, however, that any mat, no matter how small, grows increasingly uncomfortable to a cat. The longer the mat remains in the coat, the tighter it pulls, thus irritating the skin. Mats on the paw pads or between the toes probably feel a lot like having a rock in your shoe. To spare your cat discomfort, always remove mats promptly upon discovery.

Always remove any mats before bathing, too, because water will "set" them permanently and make removal more difficult. To remove a mat, separate it and work it loose with your fingers, but try not to yank on the skin. Gently pick a stubborn mat loose with the end teeth of a wide-toothed comb. Sometimes, a dab of talcum powder, baby oil, or hair conditioner helps loosen a mat, but avoid using a greasy substance unless you're going to bathe the cat afterward. If the mat is a massive tangle, clipping it out with scissors, being careful not to cut the skin, or shaving it off with electric trimmers is often the last option. Pet stores sell mat-splitters for removing stubborn tangles. A seam ripper, available at sewing supply stores, serves the same purpose. One end of the tool is hook-shaped and embedded with a tiny, single-edged blade. To cut the mat, simply slide the blade beneath the knotted hair, with the blunt edge against the skin. Be careful not to poke the skin with the tool's point. To cut, lift the tool up and outward, toward yourself, as if ripping a hem out of a garment. Separate and repeatedly cut small sections of the knot until the tangle pulls free. Obviously, you would not want to chop up a show cat's coat with these last-resort, cut-and-snip tactics; therefore, a few minutes of regular grooming once or twice a week is time well invested.

Trimming Claws

In addition to bathing and brushing, toenail clipping is something you should get your Somali accustomed to at a young age. Like your fingernails,

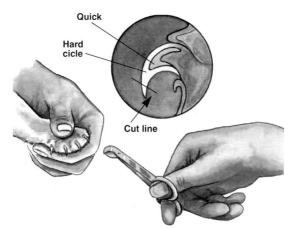

When trimming claws, clip only the white tips. Avoid cutting into the pink "quick," as this will cause pain and bleeding.

cat claws grow continuously and need regular attention. Even with scratching posts available, an indoor cat's nails do not wear down as readily as an outdoor cat's. Neglected, untrimmed claws can curve under and grow back into the paw pads, causing a painful swelling and abscess. Trim claws once a month or so and always before a show. Regular trimming reduces the risk of injury to yourself and other pets and helps prevent snags in your carpets, clothes, and furnishings.

Cats retract their claws when not in use. To extend them for trimming, hold the paw with your thumb on top and fingers on the bottom and gently squeeze. Before clipping, look closely at the nail and identify the "quick." If the nail is white, the quick clearly shows up as a thin pink line running about three-fourths of the way down the nail toward the tip. To avoid cutting into the sensitive quick, trim the nail tip below the pink line. The quick contains nerves and blood vessels, and if you accidentally cut into the pink, the cat

Before you begin bathing your Somali, assemble all of the supplies you'll need, including extra towels for drying.

When using a spray nozzle for bathing, keep the water pressure low to avoid frightening the cat.

will feel pain and the nail will bleed. If this happens, hold pressure over it with a cotton ball until the blood clots, or apply a shaving styptic.

With the cat held securely in your lap, trim the claws on the front and hind feet, starting with two or three nails at a time until your Somali gets accustomed to the idea. Use human or pet nail clippers for the job, then smooth the rough edges with an emery board or nail file. Don't forget the fifth claw slightly higher up on each inside forepaw.

Bathing Your Somali

If you are going to show your Somali, it will require a bath a day or two before the show. Otherwise, bathing a pet Somali becomes necessary only during a heavy flea season or when the coat gets oily or dirty. Remember, too many baths can rob the coat of natural oils and dry the skin, so don't bathe your cat unless it needs it.

Supplies

Different coat types demand different products to achieve that ultra-clean feel and appearance needed in the show ring. Every breeder and exhibitor has special preferences when it comes to shampoos and such, so start with what your breeder recommends. Use only products labeled safe for cats. Avoid dog shampoos, because the medication or flea insecticide in these preparations may be too strong, even fatal, for cats. Also, not all cat flea products are safe for use on kittens, so read labels carefully before applying any shampoo, spray, dip, or powder to your kitten's fur. If the label doesn't say the product is approved for use on kittens of a certain age, don't risk using it without first consulting a veterinarian. Start getting your kitten used to baths after age four months, but don't overdo it.

In addition to shampoo, other supplies you'll need for the bath include:
- a comb
- cotton balls
- a blow dryer
- towels
- a wash cloth
- a sink or tub
- a pitcher or shower spray attachment
- a source of clean, warm water for washing and rinsing

The kitchen sink is usually the ideal place for the job, but if you must bathe the cat in a laundry tub, reserve a second tub of clean water for rinsing. For blow drying the cat, you'll need a table or countertop with access to an electrical outlet. You'll probably also need a willing assistant, because most cat baths are two-person productions, especially if the feline is not fond of the idea.

Before You Start

To minimize the risk of injury to you and your assistant, trim the cat's claws first. Also before bathing, give the coat a thorough combing to remove mats or loose, dead hairs that could get tangled in wet fur.

Close off the room where the bath will take place, so you won't have to chase a wet, soapy escapee through the house. To prevent water from getting in your cat's ears, put a cotton ball in each ear, being careful not to shove them in too deeply. Before putting the cat in the tub or sink, fill the basin partially with warm (not hot) water. A rubber bath mat in the bottom prevents slipping and makes the cat feel more secure by giving it something to grip.

How to Bathe

Have your assistant hold the cat down in the partially filled water basin with gentle pressure on the back and shoulders. If the cat panics, talk to it reassuringly and gently hold it down by the scruff of the neck until it stops struggling. Be careful not to splash water in

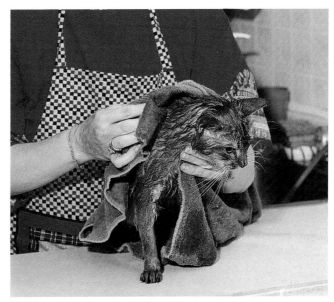

Gently press out excess moisture with dry towels.

When blow drying, use only the lowest settings and avoid blowing air directly in the cat's face.

the cat's face or dunk its head under, as this will only increase its panic.

Wet the fur first with warm water, using the pitcher to dip and pour over the cat's back. If using a spray nozzle, keep the water pressure low to avoid frightening the cat. Don't spray water directly in the face. After wetting the fur sufficiently, apply shampoo and form a lather, starting at the neck and working back toward the tail. To lather the belly, have your assistant hold up the front legs. Avoid getting soap near the face and eyes. Use a damp wash cloth or moistened cotton balls to gently wet the head and wipe the face and eye areas clean.

How to Rinse

To remove all traces of shampoo, spend twice as much time rinsing as you do lathering. Any residue left behind could make the coat look flat and greasy and cause itching and irritation. Use the spray nozzle to rinse, or put the cat in a tub of clean, warm water, then dip and pour the water from the pitcher. When the fur feels squeaky clean, drain off the water and gently press out the excess by running your hands down the back, legs, and tail. Lift the cat out of the tub or sink, being careful to support its rear end with one hand, and place it on a table or counter top for drying.

Remove the cotton balls from the ears and gently wipe away any dirt or wax visible inside the ear flap. *Never* poke cotton swabs or other objects into the ear canal, as this could cause injury to the delicate inner ear structures. If the ears appear quite dirty or exude a fruity odor, a veterinary examination is in order to rule out ear mites or fungal infections. Next, gently towel dry the sopping fur as much as possible first, changing towels as needed. Then plug in the blow dryer to finish the job.

How to Blow Dry

To prevent chilling, completely dry your Somali with a blow dryer. Towel drying alone simply doesn't take all of the moisture out of the long fur. And if allowed to air dry, a Somali's long hair may curl slightly and frizz, especially on the chest, legs, and underside. This look is less desirable for showing and is easily prevented by combing and separating the hairs as you blow dry. Like bathing, many cats learn to tolerate blow drying if you exercise some sensitivity when introducing them to the idea. Use only the low settings, never the hottest setting. Don't blow air directly in the cat's face.

To add volume to the hair, gently back-comb against the lie of the fur as you blow dry, or lift the fur with your fingers, starting at the neck and working back toward the tail. Comb the ruff on the chest upward toward the chin. Don't forget to dry the underside. Have your assistant hold up the front legs for easier access to the belly and between the hind legs. Use the brush only when the fur is almost dry; otherwise, dragging the bristles through wet fur may damage the delicate hairs.

Showing Your Somali

Most people who own a purebred cat find themselves drawn to a cat show sooner or later, if for no other reason than to see how other cats of the same breed compare to their own. Besides being the best place to meet breeders and fellow feline lovers, cat shows are fun and educational. You can learn a lot about the care and presentation of cats simply by observing how the exhibitors ready their entries for the ring and by listening to the judges' comments as they hold out and examine each cat. Large shows also attract numerous vendors that display and sell cat-motif gifts, toys, and accessories. Even if you never intend to show your Somali, attending a few cat shows will be rewarding adventures. To find out about upcoming shows in or near your area, check listings in magazines geared to the "cat fancy." The cat-registering associations also can provide information about affiliated cat shows and clubs in your area (see Useful Addresses and Literature in the back of this book).

History of Cat Shows

History credits England with staging the prototype of today's cat competitions in 1871 at London's Crystal Palace. Harrison Weir organized the show and developed the first breed standards by which the cats were judged. He became president of that country's first National Cat Club, which issued the first stud book in the late 1800s. Before long, numerous cat clubs existed in Great Britain, and the rivalry among them was intense. By 1910, the Governing Council of the Cat Fancy (GCCF) was established with delegates from the various clubs to oversee the registering of pedigreed cats and to set the rules for all cat shows in Great Britain.

In the United States, cat shows have taken place since the 1870s, but an all-breed show held in 1895 at New York's Madison Square Garden marked the beginning of real interest among North American cat fanciers. In 1899, the first and oldest U.S. registry, the American Cat Association (ACA), was formed to keep records. Today, at least eight additional cat-registering associations exist in North America. They include the Cat Fanciers' Association (CFA), the American Cat Fanciers' Association (ACFA), the International Cat Association (TICA), the Cat Fanciers' Federation (CFF), the American Association of Cat Enthusiasts (AACE), the National Cat Fanciers' Association (NCFA), the United Feline Organization (UFO), and the Canadian Cat Association (CCA). Each association has its own rules and breed standards, but all keep track of bloodlines, register cats and sanction shows. CFA, incorporated in 1919, is the world's largest registry of pedigreed cats, sponsoring approximately 400 shows a year across the United States and internationally through its more than 650 member clubs.

How a Cat Show is Organized

In Great Britain, judges go from cage to cage examining cats, and during some classes, they ask owners to leave the show hall. In the United States, however, judging takes place on tables set up at one end of the show hall in full view of all spectators

The judging ring: During a cat show class, a judge removes each cat from its cage and examines it on a table in front of interested onlookers.

and exhibitors attending. Behind each table is a row of cages, where cats entered in the same category are called by number to await judging. This setup is called a *judging ring*. A single show event may have four or more rings set up, each operating as a separate competition and presided over by a different judge. Sometimes separate clubs present back-to-back shows consisting of eight to ten rings over a two-day weekend. Cats can compete in as many rings as they are eligible for. In the ring, the judge removes each cat from its cage, places it on the table before the audience and thoroughly examines it. After evaluating all cats in the ring, the judge awards at least first-, second-, and third-place ribbons to the winners. All pedigreed cats are judged according to how closely they meet the written standard for their particular breed (see The Somali Breed Standard, pages 12–13).

The "all-breed" show. If the show is called an "all-breed" show, all cats, regardless of their type, can compete against each other. Specialty shows, on the other hand, may be restricted to longhaired or shorthaired breeds. Depending on the association sponsoring the show, various divisions and classes exist for eligible pedigreed cats, altered cats, kittens, household pets, and new breeds and colors. Unaltered, adult pedigreed cats begin their show careers competing in "open" classes against others of their breed, sex, and color. If they achieve a specified number of wins, they become a champion and can compete against other champions for the coveted title of grand champion. Many associations award additional titles beyond these.

Alter classes. Alter classes, called "premiership" in the CFA, allow spayed and neutered pedigreed cats to compete against other altered cats of the same breed. These cats are judged according to the same standards as intact cats, but instead of being called champions or grand champions, altered cats win comparable titles of premier or grand premier. Many exhibitors, particularly novices, prefer to show in alter classes, because having a "show-alter" cat relieves them of the extra commitment involved in owning a breeding animal.

Pedigreed kittens. Pedigreed kittens between four and eight months of age can compete in classes with other kittens of the same breed, sex, and color.

Household pets. The household pet (HHP) competition is for mixed-breed or non-pedigreed cats, which must be spayed or neutered. Policies vary, but some associations permit a purebred cat to be shown as a household pet, as long as the owner surrenders the papers or does not register the cat as a purebred. Exhibited as an HHP, a part-Somali, or even a shorthaired Somali sold as a pet without papers, would be judged for beauty, personality, and overall condition, rather than by how closely it fits a breed standard.

New Breeds and Colors

Most shows offer nonchampionship classes for experimental breeds and colors. Generally called Any Other Variety (AOV) or New Breeds and Colors (NBC), such classes are designed for pedigreed cats that do not conform in some way, usually in color or coat length, to their current breed standard. The first Somalis, when they were still called longhaired Abyssinians, embarked on their road to recognition in AOV classes before gaining acceptance as a separate breed.

Practices for accepting and showing new breeds, colors, and varieties differ from association to association. But in general, experimental breeds are exhibited first in non-competitive, miscellaneous, NBC, or AOV classes before being granted prechampionship, or provisional, status. Cats in provisional competition are judged according to a provisional standard, but once their new breed gains full recognition, they become eligible for championship classes.

Showing Shorthaired Somalis

To increase the gene pool for Somalis, all North American registries permit Somali outcrossings to Abyssinians, but their policies on registering and showing the inevitable percentage of shorthaired offspring vary widely. Depending on which registry sanctions a particular show in your area, a shorthaired kitten from an Aby-to-Somali mating may or may not be eligible for championship competition. For example, CFA, ACFA, ACA, and CFF require that all kittens from a Somali-Abyssinian outcrossing be registered as Somalis, regardless of coat length. This means shorthaired Somalis cannot be exhibited in affiliated shows, except perhaps as AOV Somalis or as household pets, if permitted. Not all registries permit shorthaired Somalis in AOV or NBC classes

Neutered cats like this red Somali male can be shown in alter or "premiership" classes.

either, because they do not consider them a *new* breed or variety. Even so, with no points awarded in such classes, there's little reason to enter, *except* to promote recognition for a new breed or variety.

TICA and AACE, on the other hand, allow kittens from Aby-to-Somali outcrosses to be registered and shown with the breed they resemble. In other words, longhaired kittens can be shown as Somalis, and shorthaired kittens can be shown as Abyssinians in affiliated shows. NCFA and CCA require that all kittens from Aby-to-Somali outcrosses be registered as Somalis; however, these associations devised a separate category in which shorthaired Somalis can compete for points alongside their longhaired litter-mates. The newest registry, UFO, created a similar separate championship category for showing the shorthairs and even gave them a new name, Serenti, after a city in Somalia.

Entering Your First Show

A good way to get involved in showing cats is to join a cat club in your area that is affiliated with one of the cat-registering associations. For club information and show rules, call or write the association(s) where your cat is registered. Some registries charge a small fee to cover the cost of printing and mailing their rule booklets. Your breeder also should be willing to help you get started, because your wins in the show ring will reflect favorably on the breeder's bloodlines.

If you're not involved with a club, check cat magazine show date listings, then write or call the number given for entry forms and information. Complete the entry form by the specified dead-line and return it to the entry clerk with the appropriate fee. You also may request to be "benched" next to your breeder or to someone you know who is an experienced exhibitor. Your benching assignment is the cage where your cat will stay when it's not being judged in one of the rings.

Cages and Supplies

The show flyer will list all pertinent information about the show, including the cage dimensions. Benching cages for a single cat are small, but for a little extra money, you may have the option of requesting a double cage when you send in the entry form. On the day of the show, you will need to bring some spray disinfectant to wipe down your cat's cage, plus sheets, towels, or show curtains to line the inside and bottom of the cage. Covering the cage

gives your cat a little privacy amid the show chaos and shields it from seeing the other animals in adjacent cages. It also adds an element of fun, because most shows have contests for the best decorated cage. Many exhibitors go all out to custom-design attractive cage curtains that effectively advertise their catteries.

Generally, the show committee provides a chair at each cage, cat litter, and sometimes disposable litter boxes. But you'll need to bring a small litter pan, just in case, plus your grooming equipment, a grooming table (a sturdy TV tray or plastic patio table serve the same purpose), a cat carrier, a cat bed, food and water bowls, your cat's favorite food, and any other accessories to make it feel comfortable. Of course, you will have done most of your cat's grooming at home, having bathed it a day or two before the show. Only touch-ups should be required at the show, but be prepared in case your cat makes a major mess of its fur in transit.

"Vetting"

To enter the show hall, your cat must be flea-free and disease-free. In some countries, such as Great Britain, many shows are "vetted," meaning that a veterinarian screens each cat before it is allowed inside the show hall. Although U.S. shows do not require vetting, inoculations must be up-to-date. The show flyer will state whether you must bring proof of current vaccinations for rabies or other diseases.

Judging

After you check in at the door on the day of the show and get your cat settled in its assigned cage, read the catalog schedule to determine when your cat will be judged. Listen to the public address system, and when you hear your cat's number called, carry it to the appropriate judging ring. Your number will be posted on top of one of the cages in the ring. Place your cat in the correct cage, then take a seat in the audience to watch the judging.

The judge will examine each cat in turn on the table and hang ribbons on the winners' cages at the end of the class. When the judging is over, the clerk will ask the exhibitors to remove their cats from the ring. Collect your cat and ribbons, if any, and return to your bench to await your call to the next ring. Depending on how well your cat does, it may be called back for finals, when the top contestants in a given category are presented. The highest awards at a show include Best of Color, Best of Breed, and the most coveted prize, Best in Show. Cats that win in the championship or premiership finals earn points based on the number of cats defeated at the show. These points count toward regional and national titles. To more fully understand the ribbons, points, and awards system, consult the rules booklet prepared by the cat fancy association sponsoring the show.

Traveling with Your Somali

Although your first cat show should be within driving distance of your home, traveling to the show may be a stressful ordeal for your Somali. Although some cats enjoy riding in a car, most do not. Some even get car sick. If you're going to show your Somali, get it accustomed to traveling in a car while still a kitten. Take it for short drives around the block every few days, gradually increasing the time spent in the car. For safety reasons, keep your cat in a pet carrier while traveling. This practice not only minimizes escape opportunities, it also prevents a frightened or exploring cat from getting under the gas and brake pedals or otherwise interfering with the driver's ability to control the car. In case of an accident, confining your

Cat carriers used in air travel should be well-ventilated and built of sturdy materials.

Somali to a carrier lessens the likelihood of injury from being tossed about the vehicle and reduces the risk of escape through a broken car window.

When packing, take along your cat's bed, a favorite toy, feeding bowls, food, and medications. It's also a good idea to take a gallon or two of water from home, in case your cat won't drink the different-tasting water in a strange place. The show flyer should recommend hotels that allow pets. If not, inquire in advance about the pet policy at the place where you plan to stay, and don't forget to take a litter box for use in the hotel room. If you must leave your cat alone in the hotel room for brief periods, put it in the carrier and hang out the DO NOT DISTURB sign. You don't want housekeeping personnel to enter while you're dining and let your cat accidentally slip out the door.

For long drives, set a litter box in the floor of the car and take along a harness and leash so you can let your cat out of its carrier for rest stops. Before opening the car door, always make sure your Somali is secured by carrier

Blue Somalis like this female kitten were shown in AOV classes before achieving CFA championship status in 1986.

close together or heavy wire. The remaining sides should have ventilation slots, and all ventilation sites should be protected by protruding rims to prevent obstruction by other baggage. The door latch and joints of the container must be escape-proof and impervious to biting and clawing. The container must be clearly labeled with "Live Animal" and "This End Up" and tagged with the cat and owner's names and address, plus any feeding instructions.

Some airlines allow pets in the passenger cabin as carry-on luggage, but they must remain in a special-size carrier that fits under the seat. Other airlines allow animals to be transported only in the cargo hold, and some offer special expedited delivery service for animals. Most require a health certificate issued by a veterinarian.

Although aircraft cargo holds are pressurized and temperature-controlled during flight, onboard hazards can arise during delays on the ground, before take-off and after touchdown, when the plane's compartments are not air pressurized. During that time, temperatures inside the cargo hold can fluctuate rapidly. Careful planning can help minimize these dangers when transporting an animal by air. Whenever possible, book a non-stop flight, avoid holiday or weekend travel, and avoid flying during excessively hot or cold periods.

Although tranquilizers may relieve some of your cat's travel anxiety, drugs also may make an animal more susceptible to temperature changes and breathing problems. And because sedation can have unpredictable effects in some animals at high altitudes, use tranquilizers only under the advice and guidance of a veterinarian.

Boarding Your Somali

If you're taking one cat to a show but leaving another at home, ask a trusted friend or neighbor to look in on

or leash. Because of the risk of heat stroke, never, *never* leave your Somali unattended in a parked car, especially on warm days (see page 59, first aid for heat stroke).

Traveling By Air

If traveling to a show by air, make sure your cat carrier conforms to the airline's regulations. Many pet-travel accidents are a result of poorly constructed carriers. A standard shipping carrier should be made of metal, sturdy wood, fiberglass, or rigid plastic. One entire end must be open for ventilation and covered with metal bars that are it, or consider hiring a pet sitter to care for it while you're away. Leaving your Somali in its normal environment is less traumatic than boarding it in unfamiliar surroundings at a kennel or a veterinarian's office. However, deviation from the normal household routine upsets some animals and may result in destructive behavior problems, such as defecating or urinating on furniture and carpets. If your Somali is subject to this behavior, it may be better off at a boarding facility, where it can be supervised. To lessen your Somali's separation anxiety, leave something with your scent on it (an unwashed sock, T-shirt, or house slipper) to comfort the cat while you're away.

If you decide to use a professional pet sitter or boarding kennel, ask friends for recommendations and check out the operator's references and business credentials. Inspect a boarding facility's premises for cleanliness beforehand, and ask about provisions for your cat's security and comfort. Select a kennel that houses cats in an area separate from dogs. A reputable kennel also will require proof that animals are up-to-date on all inoculations. Some will automatically dip the animal at the owner's expense if it has fleas when it is brought in.

Whatever arrangements you choose to make, leave an itinerary of where you will be and how you can be reached, and leave your veterinarian's telephone number. One obvious advantage of boarding your Somali at a veterinary hospital is that medically trained personnel are on hand to observe and handle any emergency illness your cat may experience while you're away.

Even if you're going away on an overnight trip and leaving out enough food and water in self-feeders for your cat, let someone know where you're going and when you'll be back. That someone also should have a key to your home and permission to enter and look after your cat in case you're involved in an accident that delays your return.

Breeding Your Somali

To Breed or Not to Breed

Expenses

Some people think that, because they paid $500 for a Somali kitten, they can breed their cat and make a lot of money selling kittens. If you've had similar thoughts, think again. Cat breeding is an expensive, labor-intensive hobby. First, because intact males and females tend to spray urine on their surroundings, you'll either learn to live with the smell, or you'll invest heavily in cleaning and deodorizing products, not to mention elbow grease. In addition, stud fees average about $500, depending on the male's quality, color, and show record. If the stud is a grand champion or a national winner, expect the fee to be higher, maybe as much as $2,000, because the owner has invested considerable time and money in achieving that title. Sometimes, stud owners willingly negotiate a lower fee in return for pick of the litter, but of course, this leaves you one less kitten to sell. There's also the travel costs of transporting your female cat to the stud for breeding, maybe more than once, if the mating doesn't "take" the first time.

Then, of course, there are the veterinary bills, vaccinations, cat food, advertising expenses, etc. You can't write off these expenses on your taxes unless you're operating a business. Depending on the laws in your region, you may need to purchase a business license or other special permits before establishing a cattery. Doing so may make you subject to paying state and federal taxes on your business income.

Fortunately, many people, like yourself, are educating themselves by reading books, visiting cat shows and talking to professionals *before* buying a purebred. They are learning how to avoid the "backyard" breeders and kitten mills that cruelly exploit animals for marginal profits. They've come to understand that, instead of making money, reputable breeders are more likely to invest hundreds, even thousands, of dollars in operating a cattery and campaigning their cats on the show circuit. Even after writing off allowable expenses on their taxes, most professional breeders consider themselves lucky if they break even. The real "profits" in breeding are intangible achievements, such as a Best in Show rosette, regional and national awards, and the respect of fellow cat fanciers for contributions toward perfecting the particular breed. If these goals do not interest you, leave breeding to the professionals.

Teaching Your Children

Forget the idea, too, of letting your children witness the miracle of birth by breeding your cat just once. Rent a video tape for this purpose instead. Real-life births sometimes have a way of turning into nightmarish emergencies with fatal complications that may frighten and upset children who aren't mature enough to cope with such realities. A better lesson for children is how to take responsibility for the animal lives already in this world. Teach them how proper health care, spaying, and neutering can reduce the suffering that more than eight million surplus pets endure each year. That's how many animals wind up abused, neglected, and homeless in U.S. shelters every year. Most must be humanely destroyed because there simply aren't enough homes to go around for so many. For every kitten that you bring into the world and find a home for, another one somewhere dies because it didn't get a good home. The only way to reduce this senseless waste of life is to end all indiscriminate breeding by spaying and neutering pets and by not allowing intact animals to roam freely.

Breeding Complications

For health reasons, a female should be bred only once, certainly no more than twice, a year. Somalis generally have small litters, averaging three or four kittens. This gives you few kittens to sell in a season, but on the positive side, smaller litters are a blessing. If an unborn litter is too large, the kittens may press on the mother's liver or other vital organs and cause medical complications during pregnancy.

Neonatal Isoerythrolysis (NI)

Occasional Somali litters may experience fading kitten syndrome after birth, an often-fatal condition resulting from mating individuals with incompatible blood types. This hemolytic reaction, called Neonatal Isoerythrolysis (NI), occurs when kittens that inherit blood-type A nurse from a mother with blood-type B. Type B kittens born to type A mothers are not prone to NI, because type A cats possess weaker anti-B antibodies. Blood-type B individuals, however, can have powerful antibodies against type A, and those antibodies present in the queen's colostrum (first milk) can destroy the type A kittens' red blood cells. These kittens appear healthy at birth, but they weaken and die soon afterward. Sometimes the kittens can be saved

by removing them from the mother and hand-raising them, but fostering is a grueling commitment that requires frequent, round-the-clock feedings. To prevent NI, breed type B females only to type B males. Specialized tests can identify feline blood types. Cats have three known blood types—A, B, and AB, with A the most common and AB the most rare. Research indicates that type B occurs more often in certain purebreds, including Abyssinians and Somalis, than in mixed breeds.

Getting Started as a Serious Breeder

If you're determined to get seriously involved in the cat fancy world, despite the expense and hard work involved, start with showing an altered Somali before you progress to breeding. Discover your true interests first. Talk to judges and other breeders, read books, and educate yourself about feline genetics and health care. Then, acquire the best quality female you can afford, or find an experienced breeder who is willing to co-own breeding stock with you while you serve a sort of breeder's "apprenticeship."

Most importantly, dedicate yourself to promoting conscientious cat ownership. As a responsible breeder, it will be your duty to place the kittens you produce in loving homes and make sure that the pet-quality ones are spayed or neutered. Remember, everyone who allows his or her cat to breed contributes to the pet overpopulation problem. The person who buys one of your pedigreed kittens may have given a home to one of millions of unwanted cats euthanized each year in animal shelters.

Arranging Stud Service

When selecting a suitable Somali stud, ask to see his pedigree and make sure he's a registered purebred,

Kittens are adorable, but breeding Somalis is an expensive, labor-intensive undertaking best left to experts.

virus and feline AIDS. In addition, both cats need to be free of fleas and other parasites before they are introduced.

The Sex Life of Cats

A breeding female cat is called a queen. An intact male is called a tom or stud. Ideally, a queen should not be bred until she is at least one year old, although her first heat cycle (estrus) may occur a few months earlier. Waiting a year allows the queen to achieve her full growth first, before essential nutrients must be diverted to nourish unborn kittens. A tom reaches sexual maturity between nine and 14 months, and from then on, his hormones drive him relentlessly to search for mates and to defend his territory against intruding toms. His sex hormones trigger his instinctive urge to spray and mark his territory with strong-smelling urine, which is one reason why a breeding male in a cattery typically is confined to a cage or spacious run. Neutering usually curbs this undesirable male trait, unless the habit has become well-established.

A queen comes into heat according to seasonal rhythms. The usual mating seasons come in early spring, mid-summer, and early fall. Feline reproductive cycles appear to be influenced by lengthening daylight hours, which explains why cats in the Northern Hemisphere cycle opposite to those in the southern half of the world. Most queens have heat cycles every two or three weeks during the breeding seasons; others cycle only once a month. There are many exceptions, and some cats living indoors in controlled, artificial lighting may cycle year-round.

The Heat Cycle

Except for a few queens that have "silent" heats, there's no mistaking when most females come into season. The outward signs of proestrus, the first stage of heat, include increased

preferably a champion or grand champion and preferably a proven stud that has passed on his good qualities to previous litters. If he comes from a line of champions or grand champions, those cats' names will be prefixed by Ch. or Gr. Ch. on the pedigree. Choose a male that possesses the personality traits and physical qualities you would like to see enhanced or improved in your female.

The written contract should state the agreed upon stud fee and the responsibilities of the stud owner while the female is housed in his or her cattery. Both parties should demand health certificates proving that their cats are vaccinated and free of feline leukemia restlessness and vocal calling. The queen may seem more affectionate toward her owners, rubbing against them and wanting to be petted. This stage lasts only a day or two before becoming full-blown estrus, when the queen may roll on the ground or pace from door to door. Take care to keep her in, for if the queen escapes outdoors, she may mate with more than one male and deliver a mixed litter of kittens having different fathers. The hallmark of this stage is the "call," the queen's persistent, drawn-out, throaty howl that advertises her availability to the neighborhood toms. In response to this calling, plus the high levels of sex pheromones her body produces, yowling toms from near and far line up on the fence ready to prove their worthiness as mates. To the uninitiated cat owner, this noisy experience can be quite nerve-wracking and is another good reason why spaying a female is advisable if you're not going to breed her.

Also at this stage, the queen may crouch in the characteristic mating stance, called the estrus or lordotic posture. She will assume this posture, too, if you stroke her back near the base of the tail. With front end pressed to the ground and with back hollowed, she will raise her hindquarters, swish her tail to one side, and tread up and down with her hind feet, as if marching in place. If the queen is bred and becomes pregnant, gestation normally lasts an average 65 or 66 days. If mating does not take place, she enters a stage of sexual inactivity until her next cycle begins.

The Sex Act

When your queen is ready to mate, take her to the stud. Unfortunately, traveling to strange surroundings sometimes causes a female to go out of heat, so you may have to leave her for an extended time or make more than

Red Somali kitten. A better lesson for children than witnessing the "miracle of birth" is learning how to take proper care of a pet.

Neutering or spaying your Somali will make it a nicer companion and improve its chances of living a longer, healthier life.

93

The mating game: The queen signals her readiness by assuming the mating stance.

Once the tom mounts the queen, coitus lasts only a few seconds.

Afterward, the two separate, and usually the queen rolls on her side, swats at the male, then settles down to clean herself. Soon, they will repeat the sequence several more times.

one trip to accomplish the desired goal. Generally, if the first mating proves unsuccessful, a second attempt is free. Ideally, the stud owner supervises and closely observes the mating process to ensure that neither animal gets hurt.

When all goes according to nature's plan, the queen rolls provocatively for her suitor and assumes the mating stance, inviting the tom to mount her. The tom seizes her by the scruff of the neck and proceeds to pedal with his hind legs. The brief coupling ends with a howl and a hiss from the queen as the tom withdraws. Often, she turns to swat him with her paw. The two go off by themselves momentarily to groom or to watch the other, but soon they will rejoin and repeat the mating sequence many more times.

Induced Ovulation

Cats are unusual in that they, unlike most other mammals, do not ovulate spontaneously during their cycles. Instead, they are "induced ovulators," meaning that the sex act must occur, usually repeatedly, to induce the release of eggs from the ovaries. The male penis is ridged with tiny spines or barbs that rake the inside of the queen's vagina during copulation, particularly as he withdraws. This physical stimulation of the cervix sends a message along nerve pathways to the hypothalamus and pituitary gland in the brain to release luteinizing hormone, which prompts ovulation.

Signs of Pregnancy

About three weeks after conception, the queen's nipples redden or "pink up." Her attitude may become more maternal and affectionate. Her appetite may increase, and she will gradually put on a few extra pounds. Proper nutrition is vital for the queen's health and for the developing fetuses. Your veterinarian can recommend a cat food specially formulated for reproductive needs.

Cats, like people, can suffer from morning sickness due to hormonal changes. The queen may vomit occasionally during her third or fourth week, but the problem usually lasts only a few days and requires no veterinary treatment unless it becomes severe. Report any other signs of illness to your veterinarian immediately.

The queen's abdomen becomes noticeably swollen in about a month. Resist the temptation to palpate the kittens inside, as they or the distended uterus can be injured easily. Leave this inspection to your veterinarian. For the same reason, do not allow children to pick up the queen during her pregnancy.

Basic Feline Genetics

Genetics is the science of inheritance. Somali parents pass on their breed characteristics and their individual qualities to the next generation of kittens via the genetic code contained in coiled strands called chromosomes. All body cells, except sperm and eggs, contain these chromosomes arranged in pairs. Cats have 19 pairs per cell, or 38 total. The sex cells, however, contain 19 single, unpaired chromosomes. But when egg and sperm cells unite to form a new individual, the chromosomes pair up again to total 38, bringing half of the genetic code from the father and half from the mother.

Genes

Chromosomes are made of a molecular material, called DNA (deoxyribonucleic acid), that carries the genetic code for how a kitten will look and behave. Bits of this code, such as eye color and coat length, are stored in smaller heredity units called *genes*. Genes are often called the building blocks of life because thousands of them, lined up along the chromosome strand, spell out the genetic blueprint for the entire animal. Most traits in the animal are produced by the complex organization and dynamic interaction of numerous genes. In some cases, a single gene can influence more than one trait.

Occasionally, a random change in the genetic blueprint causes a mutation in the individual that inherits the altered gene. Some mutations are bad, but others may benefit an individual by enabling it to adapt and survive better in its environment.

Because chromosomes are paired, genes for specific traits also are paired, one from each parent. This random sharing and pairing of genetic material from both parents is what allows species members to enjoy such remarkable diversity and individuality.

Alleles

Paired genes are also called *alleles*, and the gene that expresses its coded trait is said to be *dominant*. The other is *recessive*. Recessive genes can express their coded traits only when paired. For example, the gene that gives the Abyssinian its short coat is dominant, while the one that gives the Somali its longer fur, is recessive. If a kitten inherits a shorthair gene from one parent and a longhair gene from its other parent, it will have short fur, because the shorthair gene is dominant. This kitten is also said to be *heterozygous* for that trait, because it carries two different genes for it. Only a kitten that inherits two recessive longhair genes, one from each parent, will express that trait by growing long fur. This kitten is said to be *homozygous*, because it carries identical genes for that trait. The Somali, therefore, is homozygous for the longhair trait. Two heterozygous, shorthaired cats, bred together, can produce both short- and longhaired offspring; however, it is genetically impossible for two longhaired, homozygous cats to produce shorthaired kittens.

Ruddy Somali. Four possible genetic combinations produce the ruddy color.

Sex Chromosomes

The sex chromosomes determine whether the cat will be a male or a female. All females have two sex chromosomes labeled XX; males have two sex chromosomes labeled XY. When these chromosomes pair up, one from each parent, to create a new individual, an X from the mother combined with an X from the father produces a

Only one combination of recessive genes produces the rare fawn Somali.

female (XX) kitten. A male (XY) kitten results if the mother's X chromosome pairs with the Y from the father. Because only males possess the Y chromosome, the father determines each kitten's sex. Besides determining gender, sex chromosomes also can carry genes for other traits, and such traits are said to be sex-linked.

Color Inheritance

In other cat breeds, the color red (also called orange) is a sex-linked trait carried on the X chromosome. However, the color red in the Abyssinian and Somali is different and is due, instead, to the cat having inherited brown hair tips instead of black hair tips. The brown hair tips that create Abyssinian red are recessive to the dominant black hair tips that create the color ruddy. This means the gene for red can be present but hidden as long as the dominant ruddy trait is present to mask it. To be born red, a kitten must inherit the recessive brown hair tips from both parents. Rather than thinking of these traits as specific color genes—the ruddy gene, the red gene, etc.—an easier way to understand color inheritance in the Abyssinian and Somali is to visualize two genetic systems at work:

1. hair tips can be either *black* (B) or *brown* (b);

2. hair color can be either *dark* (D) or *dilute* (d).

From each system, an individual inherits two choices, one from each parent, which, in various combinations, produce the four major Somali colors:

Ruddy = Black tips and dark color
Red = Brown tips and dark color
Blue = Black tips and dilute color
Fawn = Brown tips and dilute color

Black tips are dominant over brown tips, and dark is dominant over dilute (a paler color version). Dominant traits are written in uppercase letters; recessive traits are displayed in lowercase. Because half of the traits comes from each parent, traits are written in pairs. For example a pure ruddy cat is BBDD. When you breed a BBDD cat to a BBDD, you'll always get BBDD—a pure ruddy—because there are no other genes for those traits to choose from. When you breed a BBdd (blue) to a bbDD (red), you get a cross combination of BbDd, which also is a ruddy, because the dominant black and dark traits mask the recessive brown tips and dilute color. But because this ruddy carries both recessive genes, it has the potential to produce offspring in all four colors if paired with a mate that carries the same traits. With more gene variations present from the two systems, the random recombining of those genes in each offspring, like shuffling a deck of cards, offers a greater probability of producing different colors in successive litters. Here's how it works:

The chart on page 98 shows that there are four possible genetic combinations that produce ruddy: BBDD, BbDD, BbDd, and BBDd. However, it's impossible to tell the difference simply by looking at a cat's ruddy coat. Similarly, there are two types of blue (BBdd, Bbdd), two types of red (bbDD, bbDd) and only one type of fawn (bbdd). To determine which genes your cat may carry, study its pedigree first. Its ancestors' colors will give you clues as to what recessive traits your cat may carry. Another way to tell is by the colors of kittens your cat produces.

The Somali Color Inheritance Chart on page 100 further illustrates the possible outcomes when selectively breeding the four major Somali colors.

Understanding the two systems also explains what many breeders mean when they refer to blues as being the "dilute" of ruddy and fawns as being the "dilute" of red. Silver in the Somali results from an inhibitor (I) gene that

An "inhibitor" gene imported from other breeds produces silver in the Somali, a color not recognized by all cat associations.

Somalis make good mothers. This one is trying to hold her kitten still for a good cleaning.

97

Genetic Combinations for Color

BBdd X bbDD	=	BbDd (Ruddy carrying recessive traits)
BbDd X BbDd	=	BBDD (Ruddy = black tips + dark color)
	=	BBDd (Ruddy carrying blue trait)
	=	BbDD (Ruddy carrying red trait)
	=	BbDd (Ruddy carrying red and blue traits)
	=	BBdd (Blue = black tips + dilute color)
	=	Bbdd (Blue carrying recessive brown tips)
	=	bbDD (Red = brown tips + dark color)
	=	bbDd (Red carrying recessive dilute)
	=	bbdd (Fawn = brown tips + dilute color)

suppresses the ruddy color but leaves the dark ticking. The resultant "silvering" of the agouti banding gives the Somali's ticked coat a sparkling effect. Many silvers trace back to silver-spotted British Shorthairs; others trace back to silver American Shorthairs or to silver-shaded Persians. Many more Somali colors exist in some European countries, where outcrosses to breeds other than the Abyssinian are allowed to bring in new color genes.

Breeding Strategies

Breeders attempt to concentrate a cat's good qualities by breeding it to related cats that likely carry the same desirable genes. Unfortunately, inbreeding mother to son, father to daughter, etc., concentrates any bad qualities present in the family bloodline along with the good. Linebreeding, or mating distant relatives, achieves similar results, but often with fewer detrimental effects. Frequent outcrossing to separate bloodlines of the same breed helps keep the gene pool healthy and vigorous. Where permitted by the cat fancy's governing bodies, crossbreeding, or mating cats of different breeds, can be used to increase the gene pool or to create new breeds and colors.

Importance of Shorthaired Somalis

Genetically speaking, the shorthaired Somali is a short-coated cat carrying the longhaired gene. Essentially, it is the same as a heterozygous Abyssinian, but because it carries a Somali registration number, it cannot be used in any Aby breeding program. In the United States, the Abyssinian standard prohibits outcrossing to other breeds. However, to increase the gene pool for Somalis, all U.S. registries permit Somalis to be outcrossed to Abyssinians, although their policies vary for registering and showing the predictable percentage of shorthaired kittens that result from such matings. Many demand that these shorthairs be registered as Somalis, which, in some cases, excludes them from championship competition (see the chapter, Showing Your Somali, beginning on page 83). The policy protects Aby breeders' interests by minimizing the occurrence of the longhair gene in the Abyssinian bloodlines and by preventing shorthaired Somalis from being sold as Abys. Unfortunately, the policy also makes some Somali breeders reluctant to outcross or to use heterozygous individuals in their breeding programs. Understandably, they want to avoid ending up with kittens they can't show. This is regrettable, because, aside from increasing the Somali gene pool, heterozygous short-hairs tend to improve type and color. In fact, the best Somali ticking and the longest Somali coats often seem to result in cats that have a shorthair in their recent ancestry.

Heterozygous shorthairs tend to have plushier coats than homozy-gous Abys, and although both look alike, some breeders claim they can tell the difference simply by feeling the coat. If not used for breeding, shorthaired Somalis usually are sold as pets and make equally fine com-panions as their longhaired sisters and brothers. Some associations allow the shorthairs to be shown as household pets, as long as they are not registered as purebreds.

In North America, only TICA and AACE permit the long- and shorthaired kittens from Aby-to-Somali matings to be registered and shown according to the breed they resemble. To allow them in championship competition, UFO classifies the shorthairs sepa-rately under the name "Serenti (Shorthaired Somali)." Similarly, NCFA and CCA permit long- and shorthaired Somalis in separate championship cat-egories. To make matters even more confusing, CFA groups all Somalis, whether long- or shorthaired, with other shorthaired breeds because of their Abyssinian origins and body type. This group classification is for showing and judging purposes only.

Somali Color Inheritance Chart

	Pure Ruddy	Ruddy c/Blue	Ruddy c/Red	Ruddy c/Red & Blue	Pure Blue	Blue c/Red	Pure Red	Red c/Blue
Pure Ruddy	100% Ruddy	100% Ruddy	100% Ruddy	100% Ruddy	100% Ruddy	100% Ruddy	100% Ruddy	100% Ruddy
Ruddy c/Blue	100% Ruddy	75% Ruddy 25% Blue	100% Ruddy	75% Ruddy 25% Blue	50% Ruddy 50% Blue	50% Ruddy 50% Blue	100% Ruddy	75% Ruddy 25% Blue
Ruddy c/Red	100% Ruddy	100% Ruddy	75% Ruddy 25% Red	75% Ruddy 25% Red	100% Ruddy	75% Ruddy 25% Red	50% Ruddy 50% Red	50% Ruddy 50% Red
Ruddy c/Red & Blue	100% Ruddy	75% Ruddy 25% Blue	75% Ruddy 25% Red	56.25% Ruddy 18.75% Blue 18.75% Red 6.25% Fawn	50% Ruddy 50% Blue	37.5% Ruddy 37.5% Blue 12.5% Red 12.5% Fawn	50% Ruddy 50% Red	37.5% Ruddy 12.5% Blue 37.5% Red 12.5% Fawn
Pure Blue	100% Ruddy	50% Ruddy 50% Blue	100% Ruddy	50% Ruddy 50% Blue	100% Blue	100% Blue	100% Ruddy	50% Ruddy 50% Blue
Blue c/Red	100% Ruddy	50% Ruddy 50% Blue	75% Ruddy 25% Red	37.5% Ruddy 37.5% Blue 12.5% Red 12.5% Fawn	100% Blue	75% Blue 25% Fawn	50% Ruddy 50% Red	25% Ruddy 25% Blue 25% Red 25% Fawn
Pure Red	100% Ruddy	100% Ruddy	50% Ruddy 50% Red	50% Ruddy 50% Red	100% Ruddy	50% Ruddy 50% Red	100% Red	100% Red
Red c/Blue	100% Ruddy	75% Ruddy 25% Blue	50% Ruddy 50% Red	37.5% Ruddy 12.5% Blue 37.5% Red 12.5% Fawn	50% Ruddy 50% Blue	25% Ruddy 25% Blue 25% Red 25% Fawn	100% Red	75% Red 25% Fawn

Key:

c/ = Carrying recessive

Every purebred Somali represents a substantial investment of time and money on the part of the breeder.

Raising and Selling Somalis

Preparing for Birth

Gestation, the period from conception to birth, can last from 58 to 71 days in the cat, but the average length of pregnancy is 65 or 66 days. Kittens that arrive before the 58th day may not survive, and kittens born after 71 days may be large enough to cause a difficult delivery. About a week before the expected delivery date, have a veterinarian examine the queen for signs of impending problems.

Throughout pregnancy and lactation, feed a high-protein, feline growth and reproduction diet recommended by your veterinarian. The queen's protein requirements will increase during the second half of her pregnancy, so increase her rations accordingly. Ask your veterinarian for feeding guidelines. Also, unless approved by a veterinarian, avoid giving medications to your queen or using flea preparations on her while she is pregnant and nursing. Keep her indoors, especially during the last few weeks of pregnancy.

A week or so before the due date, prepare a kittening box for her to nest in. A large cardboard or wooden box with a cut-out doorway and removable lid will do. Line the box bottom with newspapers, that can be replaced easily when soiled. Place the box in a warm, secluded, draft-free area, away from other pets and distracting noises. Place feeding bowls and a litter box nearby. Introduce your queen to the kittening box. When the time is right, her natural instincts will instruct her to rummage in closets and out-of-the-way areas of the house, looking for a suitable nesting site. If you notice this activity, show her the box, and she likely will understand what it's for and will accept it.

Some supplies you will need to assemble before the delivery include:
• a heating pad or hot water bottle for warming the nest
• an eyedropper or small ear syringe for clearing airways
• an antiseptic solution for treating the umbilical stumps
• scissors for cutting cords
• a hemostat for clamping cords or unwaxed dental floss (or thick cotton thread) for tying cords

All kittens are born with blue eyes that do not change color until about 12 weeks.

Delivering Kittens

At labor's onset, the queen may pant, cry loudly, appear restless, and purr rhythmically. She may go to the litter box and appear to strain, perhaps confusing her contractions with the urge to eliminate. If this is her first litter, the queen may appear confused and distressed about the unusual sensations she feels. Talk to her reassuringly and minimize noise and distractions. If she seems upset by your hovering presence, observe her progress from a respectful distance. But do not leave her alone until all kittens are born—if complications arise, she will need your quick assistance.

Birth is imminent when the contractions become more forceful, and the queen begins bearing down. She may lie on her side or in a half-crouching position, and she may sit up frequently to lick her vulva. A straw-colored fluid may discharge from the vulva as the water sac around the first kitten ruptures, lubricating its passage through the birth canal. From here on, things move rapidly in most cases, with kittens arriving about 15 to 30 minutes apart, although this can vary.

Presentation: Many kittens arrive head-first, but don't be alarmed if one emerges hind feet and tail end first. This seldom causes problems and occurs in nearly half of all births. However, if you see the kitten's bottom but no feet, this means the hind legs are pointing towards the head. This presentation constitutes a true breech position and can complicate labor. Call your veterinarian at once.

Amniotic Sac: Each kitten emerges either completely or partially enclosed in a grayish, semitransparent bubble, called the amniotic sac or placental membrane. Most experienced queens will instinctively strip this sac away, sever the umbilical cords and forcefully lick each kitten clean to stimulate its breathing and circulation. If she fails to do so, you will need to step in and assist by gently pinching the sac open and wiping mucous from the kitten's nose and mouth so it can breathe.

Umbilical Cord: If the kitten is breathing and wriggling, there's no rush to cut the umbilical cord. Blood passes through the cord to the kitten from the placenta. When this blood flow stops, the cord constricts. If the queen gets busy delivering another kitten and neglects to chew through the cord, simply clamp or tie it one or two inches from the kitten's navel. Then cut the cord just beyond the clamp or knot on the placental side. Dip the end in antiseptic solution. Always soak your ties and instruments in antiseptic solution before use. If using ties, trim ends short, so that only a minimal amount of string remains around the umbilical stump.

Reviving the Kitten: If the kitten isn't breathing, you'll have to cut the cord immediately so you can attempt to revive the kitten. Rub the kitten briskly with a soft cloth and clear the secretions from its face. Suck excess fluids from the airway with an eye-dropper or a small ear syringe. If that doesn't work, hold the kitten securely in both hands, firmly support the head so it doesn't flop, and sling the kitten upside down several times in a wide arc to force fluids from its respiratory passages. If the kitten still doesn't respond, blow gentle, baby puffs of air into its mouth and swing again. Once revived, warm the kitten by placing it next to a hot water bottle or on a heating pad. Put it back with the mother when she finishes delivering the other kittens.

Placentas: Throughout the delivery, count placentas carefully. There should be one delivered with or just after each kitten. A retained placenta can cause a serious postnatal infection. Also, never tug on the umbilical cord before the placenta is expelled completely. Doing so may tear the queen's uterus and cause life-threatening complications. Don't be alarmed if the queen eats the placentas, as this is her instinctive way of cleaning the nest so that predators won't be attracted by the birth odors. After delivery, remove all soiled bedding and replace with clean, fresh bedding.

Trouble Signs

In most cases, the entire litter arrives within two to six hours. On rare occasions, a queen delivers half of her litter, goes out of labor to rest, then delivers the other half many hours or even a day later. If the queen appears at ease and is happily tending to her kittens, there may be no need to worry. However, it's easy to confuse this condition with a more serious one, called *uterine inertia*, in which the contractions fade and the queen appears fatigued and uninterested in carrying on. Because a veterinarian can best judge the situation, seek medical advice if labor stops for more than two hours between kittens, especially if the queen seems weak, lethargic, restless, or anxious.

If the queen bears down purposefully for an hour without producing a kitten, or if she partially delivers one and is obviously in distress, call a veterinarian or transport her to a clinic immediately. Do not wait until she is too exhausted to deliver normally.

Small amounts of bloody or colored discharges occur normally during birth; however, persistent bleeding afterward, or any foul-smelling discharge from the vagina, is cause for alarm and may indicate internal tears or infections. It's always a good idea to have your veterinarian examine the queen after she delivers to make sure there are no retained placentas or kittens or other abnormalities.

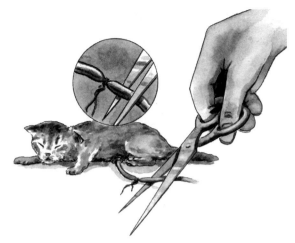

If necessary, tie or clamp the umbilical cord about one inch from the navel, then cut the cord just beyond the knot on the placental side.

Kitten Development

Healthy kittens begin suckling just minutes after birth. It's important that they nurse right away so they can ingest disease-fighting antibodies contained in the mother's first milk, called the colostrum. Born with eyes and ears closed, each kitten selects its own nipple and is guided back to the same life-giving spigot by its sense of smell. To make nursing easier for the helpless babies, keep long hair around the breasts clipped.

If the kittens cry a lot and seem fretful, they may not be getting enough milk. Depending upon the problem, a veterinarian may be able to correct it by giving the queen a hormone injection to stimulate her milk flow.

After each meal, the mother licks the kittens' genitals to make them urinate and defecate. If hand-raising and bottle-feeding kittens becomes necessary, you, too, will have to stimulate elimination by massaging their tiny bottoms with your finger.

If a kitten isn't breathing, you can clear fluids from its respiratory passages by holding it securely in both hands and slinging it upside down in a wide arc.

A healthy newborn weighs an average three or four ounces (about 100 g) and should begin gaining weight rapidly in a couple of days. If one kitten is a "runt" or appears to be gaining less weight than the others, have a veterinarian examine it.

A day or two after birth, the umbilical stumps dry and fall off the newborns. In about 10 days, their eyes begin to open. All kittens' eyes are blue at first and do not change to their adult shade until about 12 weeks of age. By 15 to 20 days old, they can crawl. Soon afterward, they can stand and toddle. By week three or four, kittens can experiment with soft, solid foods. Also by this time, they can control their own elimination, and litter box training can begin.

From three weeks on, handle and play with the kittens daily. Experts say that kittens socialized to humans at an early age grow up to be better-adjusted, people-oriented pets. At one month, kittens begin to play with each other, engaging in mock chase and combat games that will hone their hunting skills.

Supplement mother's milk with meat varieties of bottled baby food mixed with canned kitten milk (available at pet stores and veterinarians' offices). If you can't afford expensive commercial supplements, a half-and-half mixture of canned, evaporated milk and water will do, but avoid homogenized cow's milk. If food is refrigerated, warm slightly before serving. At five weeks, begin adding a balanced, commercial cat food formulated for growing kittens. By eight weeks, kittens should be fully weaned and ready to receive their first shots. By 12 to 16 weeks, they can go to new homes.

Registering the Litter

After a litter is born, the breeder sends a form and fee to the cat-registering association(s) with the breed type, birth date, sire and dam's registration numbers, and color and sex of each kitten. The registry sends back a litter registration, plus individual registration forms for each kitten in the litter. Depending on the terms of the sale, the breeder gives one individual registration slip to each person who buys a kitten. On the individual forms, the breeder completes the section for each kitten's sex, breed, eye color, coat color, etc. The buyer chooses a name, writes it in beside the breeder's cattery name (if any), completes the owner information section, and mails the individual registration form to the appropriate association(s) with the required fee.

A Breeder's Responsibility

As mentioned in the previous chapter, keep in mind that you will not make money breeding cats, after figuring in the total costs of showing, health care, stud fees, food, supplies, etc. You can, however, gain a great deal of satisfaction from knowing that you've helped create responsible cat owners by teaching buyers how to properly

The Somali standard calls for large, expressive, almond-shaped eyes, gold or green in color.

care for your kittens. When placing kittens, don't be afraid to interrogate potential buyers with questions such as:

• Do you intend to keep the new kitten indoors?
• Have you had cats before?
• Were they spayed or neutered?
• What did you feed them?
• Did they get annual medical care?
• What happened to them?
• Do you have other pets now?

Answers to these questions can reveal a lot about a person's attitude and knowledge about pet ownership. Because you decided to bring the kittens into the world, it is also your responsibility to make sure that each kitten goes to a home where it will be wanted, loved, and cared for. If you don't want the cat to be used for breeding, stipulate in a written contract (see The Sales Agreement, page 25) that the individual registration form will not be released until you receive proof that the kitten has been spayed

or neutered. Without this form, the new owner cannot register the kitten, nor can its future progeny be registered. You may include other provisions in the contract as well, barring the sale of the cat to a pet shop or research facility or requiring the cat's return if it doesn't adjust to its new home or if the new owner can no longer keep it. Have a lawyer check the wording and content of your contract before you put it to use. Often, monetary damages can be awarded if contract terms are violated.

Why go to such trouble? Each kitten you raise represents a significant financial and emotional investment on your part. The more strongly you communicate the value of this investment to potential buyers, the more likely you are to instill a similar appreciation in others. After all, one of your goals as a breeder is to educate and create cat lovers who will come to consider their Somalis as priceless companions and members of the family.

Useful Addresses and Literature

North American Cat Registries

American Association of Cat
Enthusiasts (AACE)
P.O. Box 213
Pine Brook, NJ 07058
(201) 335-6717

American Cat Association
(ACA)
8101 Katherine Avenue
Panorama City, CA 91402
(818) 781-5656

American Cat Fanciers
Association (ACFA)
P.O. Box 203
Point Lookout, MO 65726
(417) 334-5430

Canadian Cat Association (CCA)
220 Advance Boulevard,
Suite 101
Brampton, Ontario
Canada L6T 4J5
(905) 459-1481

Cat Fanciers' Association (CFA)
1805 Atlantic Avenue
P.O. Box 1005
Manasquan, NJ 08736-0805
(908) 528-9797

Cat Fanciers' Federation (CFF)
Box 661
Gratis, OH 45330
(513) 787-9009

National Cat Fanciers'
Association (NCFA)
20305 West Burt Road
Brant, MI 48614
(517) 585-3179

The International Cat
Association (TICA)
P.O. Box 2684
Harlingen, TX 78551
(210) 428-8046

United Feline Organization
(UFO)
P.O. Box 3234
Olympia, WA 98509-3234
(360) 438-6903

Somali Cat Organizations

International Somali Cat Club
10 Western Boulevard
Gillette, NJ 07933

Somali Breed Council
402 Mills Drive
Benicia, CA 94510

Somali Cat Club of America,
Inc. (SCCA)
5027 Armstrong
Wichita, KS 67204

Somali Feline Fanciers
11 Iroquois Drive
Clarendon Hills, IL 60514

Abyssinian Cat Organizations

Abyssinian Breed Council
2818 Ridge Road
Madison, WI 53705

Abyssinian Cat Club of America
4060 Croaker Lane
Woodbridge, VA 22193

Other Associations

American Humane Society
P.O. Box 1266
Denver, CO 80201
(303) 695-0811

American Society for the
Prevention of Cruelty to
Animals (ASPCA)
424 East 92nd Street
New York, NY 10128
(212) 876-7700

Cornell Feline Health Center
Cornell University College of
Veterinary Medicine
Ithaca, NY 14853
(607) 253-3414

The Delta Society
P.O. Box 1080
Renton, WA 98057
(206) 226-7357

The Humane Society of the
United States (HSUS)
2100 L Street, NW
Washington, DC 20037
(202) 452-1100

Morris Animal Foundation
45 Inverness Drive, East
Englewood, CO 80112-5480
(800) 243-2345

Pet Protection Services
TATOO-A-Pet
6571 S.W. 20th Court
Fort Lauderdale, FL 33317
Hotline: (800) 828-8667
Office: (954) 581-5834

National Dog Registry
P.O. Box 116
Woodstock, NY 12498
Hotline: (800) 637-3647
Office: (914) 679-2355

Cat Magazines
CATS Magazine
Subscriptions:
P.O. Box 420240
Palm Coast, FL 32142-0240
(904) 445-2818
Editorial offices:
P.O. Box 290037
Port Orange, FL 32129-0037
(904) 788-2770

Cat Fancy
Subscriptions:
P.O. Box 52864
Boulder, CO 80322-2864
(303) 666-8504
Editorial offices:
P.O. Box 6050
Mission Viejo, CA 92690
(714) 855-8822

Cat Fancier's Almanac
Cat Fanciers' Association
1805 Atlantic Avenue
P.O. Box 1005
Manasquan, NJ 08736-0805
(908) 528-9797

Catnip (newsletter)
Tufts University School of
Veterinary Medicine
Subscriptions:
P.O. Box 420014
Palm Coast, FL 32142-0014
(800) 829-0926
Editorial offices:
300 Atlantic Street, 10th Floor
Stamford, CT 06901
(203) 353-6650

Cat World
10 Western Road
Shoreham-By-Sea
West Sussex, BN43 5WD
England

Books
Behrend, Katrin and Wegler,
Monika. *The Complete Book
of Cat Care*. Barron's
Educational Series, Inc.,
Hauppauge, New York, 1991.

Carlson, Delbert G., D.V.M., and
Giffin, James M., M.D. *Cat
Owner's Veterinary
Handbook*. Howell Book
House, New York, 1983.

Helgren, J. Anne. *Abyssinian
Cats: A Complete Pet
Owner's Manual*. Barron's
Educational Series, Inc.,
Hauppauge, New York, 1995.

Robinson, Roy. *Genetics for Cat
Breeders*. 2nd ed. Pergamon
Press, Oxford, 1977.

Siegal, Mordecai and Cornell
University. *The Cornell Book
of Cats*. Villard Books, New
York, 1989.

Taylor, David. *The Ultimate Cat
Book*. Simon and Schuster,
New York, 1989.

Taylor, David. *You & Your Cat: A
Complete Guide to the
Health, Care & Behavior of
Cats*. Alfred A. Knopf, New
York, 1986.

Wright, Michael and Walters,
Sally, eds. *The Book of the
Cat*. Summit Books, New
York, 1980.

Additional Reading
"Providing For Your Pets in
the Event of Your Death or
Hospitalization," Association of
the Bar of the City of New York,
Office of Communications,
42 West 44th Street, New
York, NY 10036-6690. $2.00
per brochure. Enclose self-
addressed, stamped envelope.
To confirm immediate availability, call (212) 382-6695.

Right: Getting a group of lively, curious Somali kittens to hold still for the camera takes great skill and patience. (Photo courtesy of American Greetings Corporation © AGC, Inc.) Below: Somalis are fancied for their wild look, earth-tone colors, quick intelligence, and spirited personality.

Natural hams, Somalis crave attention and human companionship. The best way to keep your Somali happy, healthy, and free from annoying behavior problems is to spend time with it daily—grooming, petting, and playing with it.

Index